LLEWELLYN'S 2004 WICCA ALMANAC

MW01063011

Featuring

Elizabeth Barrette, Chandra Moira Beal,
Nancy Bennett, Boudica, Dallas Jennifer Cobb,
Ellen Dugan, Emely Flak, Ruby Lavender,
Paniteowl, Diana Rajchel, Flame RavenHawk,
Janina Renée, Laurel Reufner, Cerridwen Iris Shea,
and S. Tifulcrum

Llewellyn's 2004 Wicca Almanac

ISBN 0-7387-0307-9. Copyright 2003 by Llewellyn Worldwide. All rights reserved.

♻ Printed in the United States of America on recycled paper.

Editor/Designer: Michael Fallon

Cover Design: Gavin Dayton Duffy

Cover Images: © Digital Vision

Interior Illustrations: Don Bishop, 42, 83, 97, 103, 213, 215, 219; Kevin R. Brown, 241; Svetlana Chmakova, 191; Ellen L. Dahl, 8, 10, 15, 78, 79, 205, 208; Claudine Hellmuth, 89, 90, 222, 225, 263, 266; Matt Kenyon, 54, 56, 59, 175, 178, 195, 197; Lynne Menturweck, 30; Lisa Novak, 19, 23, 46, 273, 277; Brian Raszka, 74, 186, 234, 282, 283; Keri Smith 63, 251, 253, 257

Clip Art Illustrations: © Digital Stock; © PhotoDisc; © Corel Professional Photos; © Digital Vision; © Brand X Pictures

Special thanks to Amber Wolfe for the use of daily color correspondences. For more detailed information on this subject, please see *Personal Alchemy* by Amber Wolfe.

You can order Llewellyn annuals and books from *New Worlds,* Llewellyn's magazine catalog. To request a free copy of the catalog, call toll-free 1-877-NEWWRLD, or visit our website at http://subscriptions.llewellyn.com.

Moon sign and phase data computed by Astro Communications Services (ACS).

Llewellyn Worldwide
Dept. 0-7387-0307-9
P.O. Box 64383
St. Paul, MN 55164-0838

Llewellyn's 2004 Wicca Almanac

Table of Contents

Chapter One: Lifestyles of the Witch & Famous

Wiccan & Pagan fashions & lifestyles, media sightings, gossip & tidbits, & all things wicked & Witchy

Chapter Two: Witchcraft D.I.Y.

Do-it-yourself tips, how-tos, & empowering instructions for the very Wiccan & the extremely Witch-minded

Chapter Three: Sweep Me Away!

Tips & suggestions for Wiccans who wander through the wide & wondrous world

Almanac Section: Spring 2004 to Spring 2005

The days & the nights, the Moon & the stars, the colors & the energies,
& all the latest Wiccan/Pagan news; the yearly almanac gives you everything
you need to get you through this heady astrological year

Chapter Four: W.W.W.

The wicca-wide web

Chapter Five: Over the Cauldron

Up-to-date Wiccan opinions & rantings overheard
& spelled out just for you

Chapter Six: Eye of Toad, Ear of Newt

A Wiccan/Pagan consumer guide

Introduction

Welcome, frazzled readers of the *2004 Wicca Almanac*. We acknowledge that you may be "frazzled" because we here at Llewellyn Central tend to keep a pretty realistic eye on the culture at large. Many in our mainstream culture prefer to think that everything is "fine," smiling endlessly and wishing others "a nice day," preoccupying themselves with lots of noise and flashing lights and wondering why they're more exhausted at the end of the week than at the beginning. We are not about that at all.

In fact, we're all about acknowledgement. It's the first step in seeking help to our frazzle-itis. As a result, the *Wicca Almanac* is a collection of the best and latest thinking about living the unfrazzled life, or at least how to deal with life. Check out page 40, for instance, for tips on blending your current hip Wicca practice with a bit of yoga. Or maybe you'll like the article on page 94, on some of the blissful sanctuaries where you can find peace and calm in your own home country. All through this edition, along with yearly calendar and holiday information you will find in-depth and opinionated articles on current fashions, on Pagan art and music, on Wiccans and Witches in the media, on travel, on using the web, on Pagan festivals, and so on—all written by innovative young thinkers and expert writers on these subjects. On the whole, the *Wicca Almanac* is wholly geared to the do-it-yourself aesthetic, to young practitioners of the world's most ancient spiritual traditions who still fancy themselves independent thinkers, and to a frazzle-free lifestyle.

If, after you read this yearbook, you have some tips of your own you'd like to offer, please send them to us (at the address on page 2, or at annuals-submissions@llewellyn.com). If we like what you write, we'll publish it in the next edition of this book. And we hope you find some peace in your life in the meantime.

Lifestyles of the Witch & Famous

Wiccan & Pagan fashions
& lifestyles, media sightings,
gossip & tidbits, & all things
wicked & Witchy

Real Witches vs. the 50-Foot Pop Culture Icon

by Ellen Dugan

When Witches step out of their broom closets and interact with the world at large, they let themselves in for a wild ride. This is because while some folks take Witches seriously, others are a little nervous around them. Some folks shrug and honestly don't care about a person's religious preference, while others can't help but make smart aleck or even rude remarks to cover up their own fear or discomfort.

If I've learned anything about facing the general public and the press, it's that a Witch always must have a good sense of humor and stay humble. Do you think this is easy? Picture yourself sitting in a major

Midwestern bookstore when the announcement comes across the loud speaker: "Today in the store we have a local author, psychic clairvoyant, and practicing Witch who will be signing copies of her books . . ." Then watch everyone in the store all at one time lean out of the stacks to get a good look at the attraction.

All I could do at such a moment was sit up straighter and resist the urge to tug at the coral-colored blazer I was wearing. I took a deep breath and tried to smile reassuringly as a middle-aged woman approached. "Oh look . . ." she said, astonished. "You're normal!"

To which I replied: "Yes. I left my black pointy hat at home today." And after laughing nervously, she picked up my book and started to ask me questions about it. A few other people gathered around the table and also began to thumb through the books. One gentleman admitted, in a conspirator's whisper, that if I'd been wearing my flowing black he wouldn't have approached me.

"Yeah," a college student announced. "I guess folks think we all slink around like the character Nancy, from the movie *The Craft,* or something."

After a quiet laugh, the man pulled a small silver pentagram out from under his collar. The college student showed her goddess ring, and the first woman who approached me simply smiled, saying, "Why do most people assume that we all have a dress code?"

Overcoming Witchy Stereotypes

So, let me be the first to explain to anyone who thinks otherwise, Witches don't ride on broomsticks or fight off supernatural bad guys as they do on TV. Furthermore, Witches don't waltz around in flowing black every day. They may or may not live in huge houses perched along the coast

> One gentleman admitted, in a conspirator's whisper, that if I'd been wearing my flowing black, he wouldn't have approached me.

with meddling aunts and bunches of black cats in attendance. To my knowledge there is no such thing as the "death watch beetle," and I gave up walking on water last year for Lent (ha, ha).

So where did all of these silly stereotypes come from? From popular culture of course.

The fact is, many people only know about Witches from what they have read in a book, seen on television, or at the movies. Sometimes, these are positive and powerful images, and sometimes they're the opposite. Still, I find often that when people start to ask me questions about Witches that reveal their reliance on popular culture stereotypes, they don't mean any harm really. They are simply looking for a starting place to learn about something that is foreign to them.

If you snipe at people for asking such questions—and sometimes it's really hard not to—you will lose the chance to make a positive influence on them and on their opinion of you and of Witches in general.

My personal favorite question is when someone asks me if I am like Phoebe on *Charmed,* because I am clairvoyant as well as a Witch. On such occasions, I take a deep breath and answer them back with a bit of humor, letting them think about how silly their question is. It only takes a little forethought to be able to turn a rude remark or silly question to your advantage. And with luck, perhaps you can do some good work by turning a misconception or frightening idea into the truth.

Popular Culture, Popular Questions

Bewitched

This 1960s television show seems to be a favorite starting point for popular culture type questions. It may seem silly to a modern Witch, but many people's "knowledge" of witchcraft starts first and foremost with Darren and Samantha.

So this means I'm always hearing such questions as: *Does your husband know? Does he mind, or is he a Darren?*

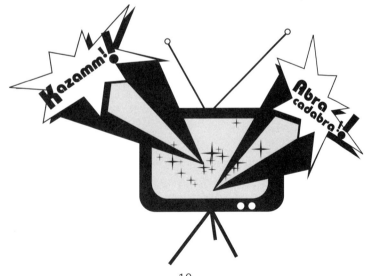

Well yes, I answer, my husband knows that I am a Witch, and has from the beginning of the relationship (twenty-two years ago). And no, he does not get grumpy if he finds out that I've done magic.

Are all of your children Witches?

Quite frankly, I reply, that will be up to them. They were raised by a mom who is a practicing Witch, so to them this is no big deal. It's simply part of who they are. But I've left it up to them to decide what they want to be. My daughter does practice, and my sons have both participated in Sabbat celebrations. I would trust any of them to call a quarter or help me with a magical project without hesitation.

Do your neighbors spy on you?

No, I do not have meddling neighbors like Mrs. Kravitz. I am discreet and have a great six-foot-tall privacy fence. Out of respect for others, I try to keep rituals and gatherings as low-key as possible. To the average person looking on, all they would see is a gathering of friends.

Can you really twitch your nose and make things happen?

Wouldn't that be nice? If I ever figure out how, I'll let you know. It sure would come in handy when faced with the massive amounts of laundry three kids can generate.

The Craft

This movie has caused a great deal of dissension among Wiccans and Pagans. Whether you loved the movie or hated it, many folks were introduced to the idea of young female Witches through this movie. So take a deep breath, find your sense of humor, and tackle this topic head on.

Can you do that glamour thing to your hair and eyes?

No, I reply, not without a box of hair color or colored contacts. But this power sure would make life simpler, wouldn't it? I see a little gray coming in so, zap! Instant hair color. But in reality, glamour is really a way of making people see you in a different light. It only changes the perception of you, not your physical

11

appearance. Glamouries can backfire easily. So, you should be careful how you use a glamour, or you could attract attention from unwanted people.

Where can I find a magic shop like in the movie?

Simple. Just look in the Yellow Pages under Metaphysical or New Age Retail Shops. Or just ask around. Most communities have a favorite magical shop, or several places full of magical supplies. If you can't find anything locally, then try the local arts and crafts store. No kidding. Many types of candles, dried flowers, and essential oils can be found there. Check out a spice shop for potpourri supplies, or a garden center for plants and herbs to plant in your garden or in containers. Magical supplies are natural and simple. They are readily available, and all around you.

Have you ever had another Witch attack you?

As in the movie? Nope. No snakes in the bathtub or flying girls bursting in through windows. Have I ever had a falling out with a magical friend? Yes. And as in any other instance when friends break up, it can be dramatic and painful, with misunderstandings and hurt feelings all around. Sometimes the breakup is for the best, or it can be just be a sad situation, occurring because no one would bend or take time to straighten out a misunderstanding. You live and learn just like anyone in such a situation.

I learned a lot from this movie. Are there any others like this one that you could recommend?

Yes, *The Craft* was a fun and entertaining movie. But it was also make-believe, and not a "training film." Repeat after me. *The Craft* is not a training film. Instead, I recommend that you go to the library or the bookstore and crack open some books on Wicca, Goddess worship, and natural magic to start learning the true nature of the craft.

Sabrina and Harry Potter

Sabrina the Teenage Witch has been popular as a children's television show for years. Cute, silly, and harmless, it is very popular with younger girls. At the same time, unless you've been living under a rock, you know all about Harry Potter series, and how these books and films have impacted children and adults worldwide. Both are wonderful and imaginative stories; however, because of their impact children often have created certain expectations of Witches and wizards. When they actually meet a Witch, who appears as an ordinary person, they are a little crestfallen.

It's important to answer a child's question about the craft honestly and as gently as possible. When my elementary-aged nieces and nephews ask me questions about Witches and wizards, I use humor and terms they can comprehend. No matter what, I talk to them as intelligent, but younger, people.

So, is your daughter just like Sabrina, or is she more like Hermione?

In some ways she is like both of these fictional characters, and in others she isn't like either of them at all. My daughter lives at home, with her family, in a normal house in the Midwest. She does not live away at a magical boarding school in England, or on the east coast with her two aunts in a massive house complete with a magical linen closet.

Yes, she is a teenage Witch. And she lives her life, loves her family, goes to high school, and hangs out with her friends. She is determined, talented, and studies hard to learn the craft.

Do you have a black cat, and does your cat talk?

Our family has two cats—a gray and black tabby, and young black cat. Do they talk? Well, they chirp and meow, just like any other cat. They are most vocal when they want to romp in the garden or to have their food bowl filled. But they won't answer questions with anything more than "meow."

Does a real Witch do spells on her classmates?

No, they do not. Witches believe that casting a spell on someone without permission is unfair and unethical. Real Witches believe in the principle of "harming none." Love spells are considered manipulative, mean, and sneaky. And nasty magical tricks to get even only result in a return of such energy against you. To my knowledge my daughter has never turned herself into a cat, or had any spells blow up—at least not so far.

Practical Magic

This is another fun movie that has inspired a lot of questions. I'll never forget when I saw this for the first time with a friend who kept asking throughout the movie, "Is that real?" I tried not to laugh and quietly answered no.

Then the scene of dancing naked under a Full Moon happened. Again, she leaned over to ask me, and I smiled and said, "Well actually, yeah. That is real."

She did a double take, and her mouth dropped open. "Oh," she replied in a very small voice.

"And you always wondered how my roses got so big . . ." I teased. Her response was to throw popcorn at me.

Anyway, on to more questions.

Can magic really be inherited from generation to generation?

Actually, just as with blue or brown eyes, psychic ability or artistic talents, magic can be passed down. It's up to the person who inherits to choose what to do with it. A gift can be left unwrapped and ignored, or opened up and cherished. However, I do not recommend that you try to conjure up a familiar anytime soon.

Can a circle of women, as was shown in the movie, really cast out a ghost?

Probably, they could—if they knew what they were doing. I'd be darned careful though. A group of people focused on one goal, with positive intentions in mind, can accomplish wonders, but you never know what you're up against in such cases.

Buffy the Vampire Slayer and Charmed

These are two popular modern television shows that inspired a whole new generation to learn more about the craft and magic. The problem is it is difficult to convince folks that much of the what occurs in these shows is Hollywood fantasy, and not real.

If I become interested in witchcraft, will my sexual orientation change?

No, it will not. Please realize that your religious beliefs will not affect your sexual orientation, whatever it may be. Know, though, that Witches and Pagans tend to be an open-minded bunch, as a rule. That is, we do not discriminate on the basis of race, gender, or sexual preference.

14

I don't know anything about demons and vampires. Can I still become a Witch?

Actually, Witches do not associate with evil or work with demons in any way. Witches don't even believe in a devil. As to vampires, well, that could open up a whole can of worms. Real vampires, as depicted in the Dracula movies, don't exist. Psychic vampires and vampire wanna-bes, however, abound. In the seventeen years I have been practicing, I have never encountered a blood-sucking vampire or demon, only relatives who could put them to shame.

Can a Witch really stop time or blow things up?

A Witch cannot "freeze" time. This is one of those things that in Hollywood is filed under special effects. I have heard of Witches working magic to get to where they are going on time. But other that that, nope.

As to blowing things up, I do know of a few magical folks who tend to have light bulbs that short out whenever they are upset, angry, or stressed out. While that sounds pretty cool, it can be a pain when you have to keep buying new light bulbs all of the time. (Just ask my family).

Is the Book of Shadows real, and do all Witches have them?

A Book of Shadows is simply a magical journal of spells and charms that a Witch keeps handy. I have seen folks use their computers, or a three-ringed binder, or a blank book for this. Think of a magical cookbook or a Witchy "scrapbook." One lists their tried-and-true spells in a Book of Shadows, along with journal entries, notes, and photos or favorite artwork.

Is there really such a thing as the "Power of Three"?

There is a craft belief that whatever magical energy is sent out by a Witch, whether it is good or bad, will return to its sender "times three." It is not uncommon for Witches and other users of magic to end a spell with the phrase, "By all the power of three times three, as I will it, so shall it be." This is a way to bind the spell, or finish it. By saying this, the practitioner is verbally reinforcing that they accept the idea of karma, and they are working to "harm none."

So, there you have it. These questions and answers ought to give you a running start and lots of creative ideas about how to deal with common stereotypes based on popular culture. Just remember, keep your answers light and maintain a sense of humor. Most folks don't have any idea what to make of a "real" Witch. As a default, they rely on what they have read or seen on TV or in films.

If you answer the questions with panache and wit, people will remember you in a positive way. Give folks the benefit of the doubt. They want you to tell them the truth. Give it to them straight, and encourage them to read more about the topic on their own.

The truth is out there . . . (Ha! Another pop culture reference).

The Magic Pen
Pagan Themes in Contemporary Literature
by Elizabeth Barrette

When I first started studying the topic of Pagan literature, hardly anyone else knew what I was talking about. "Pagan literature," they would say, "what the heck do you mean by that?"

I tried to explain, and gradually I got better at it. But more importantly, the field itself began to grow by leaps and bounds. In time, there were more examples—some very popular. All of a sudden, people just caught on without my having to explain it.

This article introduces many novels and short stories that feature Pagan themes or characters. I skip the most famous ones in favor of showing you the ones you might otherwise miss. People have written whole books analyzing the works of J. R. R. Tolkien and J. K. Rowling; look there if you want to study those stories. There's a great deal of territory beyond Hobbiton and Hogwarts, so get ready to have an adventure.

The Appeal of Pagan Fiction

Why is Pagan fiction so common now? Well, I think it's about far more than mere entertainment—though quality fiction should always entertain as it enlightens, Pagan stories do many things for us. Tales of the gods give us a chance to explore theology and why we practice as we do. They ask questions, such as: Who or what are the gods, anyway? Why do we worship them? What do we give them, and what do they give us in return? How do ethics apply to both mortals and immortals?

Pagan literature, in all its varied forms, holds a mirror up to our lives. How do we live in today's world? How did we live in the past?

Tales of magic make us think about our own ritual work, and whether we approach it as spirituality or spellcraft. We ask ourselves who bears the responsibility for a spell's results? What distinguishes positive or "white" magic from negative or "dark" magic? How much of magic happens in our minds, and how much in the outer world? If you had access to a lot of magic, what would you do with it?

Tales of heroes challenge us to consider our own greatness. What do you find worth fighting for, dying for, or living for? Who holds your loyalty? What does "honor" mean to you? What kinds of valor inspire you the most? If the universe called on you to behave as a hero, how would you respond?

Pagan literature, in all its varied forms, holds a mirror up to lives. How do we live in today's world? How have we lived in the past, and how might we live in the future? What forms and transmits our culture? What challenges face us and define us? How do we deal with others who follow a different path?

How do we live in today's world?

Throughout history, people have come together in different groups, often in search of spiritual expression. The modern Pagan movement, while drawing on many ancient traditions for inspiration, is relatively recent in formation. Religion, like any spiritual phenomenon, can be reincarnated anew in different eras. Each subculture needs a way of creating and describing its traditions and whatever gives it a unique flavor. One such tool is literature. We have women's literature, gay literature, Jewish literature, etc. Stories have been told among certain groups for ages, yet in contemporary times have found new life and cohesion. So, too, is the case with Pagan fiction.

Some of the following stories were written by, about, and largely for Pagans. Others were written by non-Pagan authors who might have known little or nothing about Pagans but drew inspiration from Pagan sources. What unifies these stories is more than a sense of wonder, it is a sense of reverence—even in those stories where the plot turns dark or mocking. Pagan fiction evokes in us a feeling that magic and divinity are potent, meaningful forces that we can explore to our own benefit.

These stories offer more than just idle entertainment. They demonstrate that the real magic lies in the square millimeter where pen meets paper.

Stories with Pagan Themes

Most Pagan tales take place in other worlds or in magical versions of ours. They touch on Pagan motifs in various ways—sometimes in magic, other times in cosmology. They give us a chance to imagine reality painted over in brighter colors. They invite us to dream.

Several novels take classic ideas in magic and develop them into an entire storyline. *Challenges* by Sharon Green and *New Moon* by Midori Snyder both feature a system based on the elements. In Green's novel, characters endowed with powers of earth, air, fire, water, and spirit must band together to take over a magic-based government. In Snyder's novel, Jobber and friends live on the street, hiding from government officials who want to kill everyone who exhibits a trace of magical power.

Another famous motif, the familiar, reaches its pinnacle in Philip Pullman's novel *The Golden Compass*. Here each character has a daemon—a creature tied to them body and soul. The daemons shapeshift during childhood but eventually "settle" on a single adult form suited to their person's nature. Also noteworthy is a unique magical artifact, the wondrously confusing alethiometer that makes little sense to anyone until the girl Lyra discovers that she can intuitively use it. Alan Dean Foster also uses the familiar motif, but places it in context of a sentient planet called *Midworld.* What is more Pagan than thinking the world that sustains you is alive, intelligent, and connected to you through your very own familiar (here called a *furcot*)? When strangers arrive and attempt to exploit the planet's riches, Midworld and its people fight back. The result is messy, but magnificently engrossing.

In fantasy, a classic quest involves saving someone or something from the forces of darkness. Charles de Lint, famous conjurer of numinous tales, sweeps us away with *Greenmantle.* In order to rescue her friends, Mally must figure out how to summon the Mystery, who can appear as man or stag or curious mixture of both. Tanya Huff opens a different can of worms in *Gate of Darkness, Circle of Light.* Here, several of her characters manifest aspects of the Goddess—Maiden-Warrior, Mother, and Crone. They wind up saving the world with the help of an Adept of the Light, a novice bard, and a tomcat who turns out to be more than "just a cat."

In *So You Want to Be a Wizard,* Diane Duane demands from her characters nothing less than the saving of the universe. The Lone Power has stolen the Bright Book in which all things are named, and the other Powers bestow magic upon young wizards to protect Life. George R. R. Martin takes us to a strange land of long, carefree summers and longer, savage winters haunted by undead marauders and worse. Magic, faith, and simple loyalty offer glimmers of hope against the chill as the characters play *A Game of Thrones.* Stories like these remind us to be valiant in the face of darkness, be it petty or mighty.

Many fantasy novels qualify as nominally Pagan simply by including a polytheistic cosmology. I favor stories that go a little farther than this. Jonathan Fesmire's novel *Children of Rhatlan* takes place in Taibril, a world guarded by two gods, Lothay and Rhatlan, and a goddess, Moreri. Rhatlan's special concern is the status of "duals," magical twins sharing minds and bodies who can only manifest in the physical realm one at a time. The main characters, Garum and Vayin, are a brother-sister pair struggling to overcome a widespread prejudice against them.

The Curse of Chalion by Lois McMaster Bujold features five deities—Daughter of Spring, Mother of Summer, Son of Autumn, Father of Winter, and the Bastard—recognized by only some of the characters and respected by none. With their help, Cazaril must figure out how to lift a terrible curse on his country, and how to get rid of the demon inadvertently trapped inside his own body. James Alan Gardner's *Commitment Hour* features deep and thoughtful theological discussion, as Fullin explains how the gods—Master Crow and Mistress Gull—can work miracles through mundane things like airplanes. It gives a whole new meaning to the idea of "faith."

Goddesses take the lead role in some fantasy religions. Consider the backstory about Sintia, the home planet of Priscilla Mendoza in *Conflict of Honors* by Sharon Lee and Steve Miller. Though exiled, Priscilla trained as a priestess of the Goddess and still wields formidable magic. Mercedes Lackey presents the four faces of the Goddess as Maiden, Warrior, Mother, and Crone in the Dhorisha Plains. Tarma shena Tale'sedrin is a swordsworn priestess of the Warrior, pledged to avenge the slaughter of her tribe.

In Patricia Kennealy's novel *The Silver Branch,* we meet Aeron Queen of Kelts out among the stars (that is, not on Earth). As a Ban-draoi (woman-druid) priestess, Aeron speaks with the goddess Dana, but she also holds the power to destroy the entire planet of Bellator in retribution for her slain kin. Like the Fair Folk of legend, this tale has a terrible beauty. These books show that the Goddess is not gentle in all her guises.

Some Pagan stories deal with deities known to our world. Turned loose in fiction, they wreak rather more havoc than we tend to see in our everyday life. In Andre Norton's

Moon Mirror, the Alathi call upon the divine by many names—Isis, Astarte, Bast, and so on. She also rephrases "The Charge of the Goddess." In *The Last of the Renshai,* Mickey Zucker Reichert presents a race of terrifying warriors who follow the Norse gods. Because the Renshai dismember slain enemies (as everyone thinks, wrongly, that this will prevent those souls from reaching Valhalla), other tribes unite to destroy the tribe. Jamie Freeman offers an insightful retelling of Greek mythology in her story *Pandora,* wherein the goddesses conspire to turn Zeus' destructive ways to a better, more productive purpose.

But wait, there's more . . .

Stories About Actual Pagans

A newer phenomenon is the rise of fiction which features Pagan characters. Most examples of this, especially those dealing with contemporary characters, settings, and challenges, are quite recent. This is the cutting edge of Pagan fiction, and you don't want to miss it. Here we get to see characters who, in various ways, are like us and may face some of the same problems we do. These stories make us think.

One popular subgenre of this trend is historical fiction. Given that much of history took place in Pagan times, this means historical novels involve Pagan characters. Some authors gloss over this, while others describe these elements in loving detail. Jean M. Auel, who almost single-handedly launched the "prehistorical fiction" movement, does some of her best work in *The Mammoth Hunters.* Based on genuine archaeological finds, Auel creates the Mamutoi, a tribe of Ice Age hunters who honor the Great Mother as the source of all life. Mary Mackey's *The Year the Horses Came* has a similar tone, though the novel is set a bit later than Auel's. This story captures the moment when a peaceful Goddess-worshipping culture meets a man from a violent God-worshipping culture; thus two utterly different Pagan religions, each with its own power and intrigue, meet.

Jennifer Reif's tale of ancient Greece, *Aphrodite's Riddle,* involves a young priestess named Aila who must solve the mystery of missing artifacts. Aphrodite herself appears in this delightful story that weaves romance and adventure. Lisa Croll DiDio brings us *Sherwood Forest* as we've never known it before, beginning when Robin and Maid Marian meet in a wild Beltane rite. This novel captures the passion of primal religions in early civilization.

Some authors venture to explore worlds just a half step from our own. In *The Pillars of the World,* Anne Bishop pits Inquisitors against Witches in the mortal world, as the Fae frantically try to discover why their own world is unraveling. Uplifting and terrifying, this story takes a close look at magic and loyalty. *The Jigsaw Woman* by Kim Antieau spans centuries and continents, following a small group of people as they repeatedly incarnate together, struggling to free themselves from a web of violence and betrayal. The glimpses of Goddess-centered cultures are exquisite.

The most recent branch of the modern Pagan genre deals with Wiccan or other Pagan characters in a contemporary setting, with or without magic involved. Starhawk's novel *Walking to Mercury* involves self-discovery, as activist Maya Greenwood seeks to reestablish her connection to the divine powers she calls "the Eternals." It carries much the same eco-feminist flavor as the author's nonfiction books, especially *The Spiral Dance,* a book that helped launch the modern Pagan movement. *In the Land of*

Winter by Richard Grant concerns a Witch's fight to retain custody of her child, a very real concern in today's world. Isobel Bird taps into the blossoming interest in witchcraft among younger people with her series *Circle of Three*. In the first book, *So Mote It Be*, three high-school girls discover that magic doesn't always work as expected as their spells go haywire. They have to work together to straighten out the mess they've made.

> We get to see characters who, in various ways, are like us and may face some of the same problems we do. These stories make us think.

Two leading voices in Pagan fiction today are M. R. Sellars and Alex Bledsoe. Sellars writes a series of mystery-thriller novels featuring a Wiccan, Rowan Gant, as the protagonist. As introduced in *Harm None,* Rowan has modest magical powers and gets drawn in more for his knowledge of Wiccans and the religion. As the series progresses, he gains more ability, and fascinating weirdness results. Bledsoe writes short stories about Tanna, the "Firefly Witch," who is blind by daylight but magically endowed with sight in the presence of fireflies. Also featured is her husband Ry Tully, a newspaper reporter. The stories cover everything from the challenges of living Pagan in a small town to dealing with supernatural beasties. *PanGaia* has published several stories, including "Croaked," a blend of folklore and mystery.

Some authors enjoy matching Pagan characters with fantasy characters. Mercedes Lackey pairs a Witch with a vampire in *Children of the Night.* Here, the two characters try to stop a soul-eater. Despite the "horror" elements of the story, this is actually a lot of fun. Gael Baudino strikes a more haunting note in *Strands of Sunlight,* in which she pairs a Wiccan with a band of elves. The immortal elves, made "to help and to heal," have lost their Goddess amidst the dreary depression of modern life. It falls to Sandy Joy and Wiccan magic to find her again.

Sometimes the stories turn really dark. In "Cancer Alley" by Nancy A. Collins, Homer Marsalis uses African magic to raise his dead family so they can talk to the company whose toxic waste killed them. Still, dark doesn't always mean depressing. Paul Edwin Zimmer spins a tale of gripping heroism in "The Hand of Tyr," notable for its handling of Norse cosmology. One of the Einherior reincarnates as a mortal man so that he can stop a band of renegades from setting off an atomic bomb. In the end, he gives his own life—just as Tyr sacrificed a hand to bind Fenris Wolf. Raven Kaldera invokes the power of Annwn in "Hands of a Dark God," in which the characters practice willing sacrifice in a ritual of erotic torture. Each of these tales confronts Death in a different way, using Pagan imagery to explore something largely ignored in American culture. Any of them would make excellent reading for a Samhain discussion.

Accidental Pagan Stories

Now we come to stories of people who don't necessarily mean to be Pagan, but find themselves caught up with deities or magic or other strangeness. In "Chatting with Anubis," Harlan Ellison illustrates the danger of disturbing a god. Sheri S. Tepper infuses *The Family Tree* with an odd rendition of Paganism that includes a Maiden Priestess as the Goddess incarnate and an odd Tree that talks to the main character as it quietly begins taking over the world. "Welcome the Medicine" by Marybeth O'Halloran touches on Native American tradition. In this story, a woman who never showed much interest in magic suddenly finds a need for it, becoming again the healer she had been in previous lives.

Perhaps the sweetest of these stories is Doranna Durgin's novel, *A Feral Darkness*. It begins during Brenna's childhood, when she offered a heartfelt prayer to the dog-loving god Mars Nodens, a patron deity who later reappears in Celtic guise as Nuadha. Though raised Christian, Brenna later discovers other options that suit her better. She needs the magical support, and she takes a whimsical approach that seems to fit.

All of these stories pluck at the common threads of contemporary Paganism, where most people have come to their path by chance rather than by upbringing.

In all its forms, Pagan literature beckons us beyond the borders of our everyday world. It reminds us why we choose to live a magical and spiritual life. It gives us good examples to follow and bad examples to avoid. It helps us tell people who we are and what we do, and it lets us celebrate our deities and beliefs and practices.

Most importantly, Pagan stories encourage us to try our own hand at storytelling. So pick up the pen. What tales do you want to tell?

What a Doll!
Barbie as Latter-Day Goddess
by Elizabeth Barrette

During my childhood, I had little interest in Barbie dolls. That changed when I grew up and had a life-altering experience.

One day, I wandered into a specialty toystore where I spied a pair of spectacular dolls billed as "Goddess of the Sun" and "Goddess of the Moon." *Was I really seeing the word "Goddess,"* I wondered, *on the box of a Barbie doll?* Yes, I had read the label correctly: a world-famous toy company had used the G-word on one of their most successful product lines.

So I gave up my earlier view of a boring and conventional Barbie. In fact, she's come a long way, picking up some interesting occupations and accessories in the process. Who would have expected the original "Material Girl" to add magic and divinity to her shopping bag? Yet she has, and the results are nothing short of fascinating.

The Evolution of Barbie

Like Athena from the head of Zeus, Barbie sprang from the fertile imagination of someone named Ruth Handler. Ruth watched her daughter Barbara (for whom the doll is named) dressing up paper dolls. Because young Barbara did not care much for baby dolls, Ruth surmised that she

> I gave up my earlier view of a boring and conventional Barbie. She's come a long way, and picked up some interesting occupations and accessories in the process.

might prefer a more glamorous teenaged doll. The model for Barbie's bombshell shape came from "Lilli," an adult doll intended for German men.

Ruth took these concepts and came up with the first Barbie doll in 1959. Barbie #1 had fair skin and either blond or brown hair. She wore a zebra-striped swimsuit, and shoppers could acquire twenty-two other outfits for her. Barbie went through some changes over the years, and gained variety in both coloring and wardrobe. She also picked up friends and family, and today the supporting cast of dolls is vast.

Collectors refer to two eras for Barbies—the vintage era (1959–1972) and the contemporary era (the late 1980s to the present). The interim period, between 1972 and the late 1980s, is discarded for its inferior dolls. Today's market for both periods is lively. The contemporary period boasts a number of dolls with amazing associations.

Goddess Barbies

A survey of Mattel products shows ten Barbie dolls with the word "Goddess" in their official titles. Some of their descriptions

specifically acknowledge the influence of one or more historic goddesses. Others show an amalgam of cultural motifs. All of them are magnificent.

I was particularly pleased to see designers taking the title seriously, in that every Goddess Barbie shows attention to detail and sumptuous trappings. Most belong to a Limited Edition or Collector Edition series. These dolls truly live up to the long-standing Pagan tradition of adorning the effigies of a goddess.

So step inside Barbie's Dream Temple and meet these ladies of luxury.

"Goddess of the Sun," aka "Sun Goddess" (1995)
This doll belongs to the Bob Mackie Designer Series. She wears a glorious golden gown decorated with more than 11,000 beads and sequins. Its collar flares into solar rays around her head. Rhinestones add flash to the headpiece that holds her golden hair in a regal style. She also boasts matching Sun earrings. This radiant Barbie reminds me of goddesses such as Sunna and Amaterasu.

"Goddess of the Moon," aka "Moon Goddess" (1996)
This doll belongs to the same series as the aforementioned Bob Mackie doll, but she is the dark sister of Sun Goddess Barbie. Her sheath dress, replete with midnight-blue sequins, peeks out from beneath a starry cape. A pointed blue hat holds her hair but reveals crescent earrings. She grasps a large crescent Moon and looks every bit the powerful enchantress. She makes me think of dramatic lunar goddesses—Diana, Hecate, and Selene.

The Classical Goddesses Collection
This series of dolls draws its inspiration from ancient Greece and Rome. The description for "Goddess of Beauty" (2000) names both Venus and Aphrodite as sources. She wears an outfit comprised of a gown, toga, and draperies in white and pale blue accented with Greek patterns in gold. She wears her dark hair in a traditional style, swept up to cascade back down in long spirals.

"Goddess of Spring" (2000) has more obscure antecedents. She wears a lavender gown and overskirt bordered with grapevines. She carries bouquets of flowers, with more adorning her loose golden hair. A golden necklace continues the floral theme. Her accoutrements suggest connections with Anna Perenna, Flora, Hebe, Kore, Maia, and Vesta—the Greeks and Romans were thoroughly enamored of spring goddesses.

"Goddess of Wisdom" (2001) has a more formidable look. She wears a pleated gown of golden fabric, its bodice looped with creamy chiffon and fastened with a golden medallion. Over this drapes a creamy cape accented with Greek patterns in gold. She has sandals, as a Greek goddess should, and golden earrings. She also wears a crown of golden laurel leaves. Her dark hair hangs to her ankles in two heavy ropes. Although not explicitly named in the doll's description, there can be no doubt that this is Athena/Minerva, for she bears her most definitive emblem. Alighting on her antique gold-tone wrist cuff is an owl, her companion symbol of great wisdom.

The Great Eras Collection

A more whimsical rendition of Athena is found in the "Grecian Goddess" (1996) of the Great Eras Collection. She wears a white pleated tunic decorated with gold laurel leaves and a pink-purple cloak with a Greek "key" design worked in gold and white around its border. Under this she has iridescent sandals. More laurel leaves adorn the headdress that holds up her curly blond hair. Several places in her description indicate her identity; she is "Protector of Ancient Athens. Goddess of wisdom . . . fashioned after the goddess Athena." This doll bridges the concepts of a stern traditional goddess and a modern lighthearted Barbie.

The International Beauties Collection

For these dolls Bob Mackie does not draw on any specific goddesses, but rather on regional motifs. "Fantasy Goddess of Asia" (1998) piles her black hair high atop her head. She wears a slim gown of green, cream, and cranberry with a sheer bodice worked in beads. A dramatic green dragon romps across the fan that rises behind her head and shoulders. She also carries a smaller fan in her hand, whose red and gold colors suggest the Japanese flag and the solar emblem of Amaterasu. She reminds me of goddesses such as Hsi Wang Mu, Toyo-Uke, and Chang-O.

Sadly, this doll has drawn protests from some Asian women, who suggest she is obviously designed to satisfy the white male gaze that has promoted "trafficking of Asian women" by legitimizing industries such as the mail-order brides. I find this idea difficult to support given the symbols of power in the doll—most notably the dragon, but also the colors red and gold—but perhaps Asian women may see something in this that I don't. I thought it lovely that Asian girls now have a Goddess Barbie to dream about; Mattel has done a fine job in recent years of issuing Barbie in diverse skin tones, hair and eye colors, and ethnic outfits, and this seems to fit into that attempt.

Another example of this is the "Fantasy Goddess of Africa" (1999), who wears a snug gown rich with embroidery and beadwork and whose hemline flares out into a circle. Black, white, orange, and burgundy twine in circles and lines all down the dress—a showy display of traditional African colors and patterns. Beaded forearm cuffs match the gown. Even more stunning is her wheel-neckpiece of gold hoops and colored threads. She also sports a tall headdress of flaming orange feathers supported by more gold hoops. Particularly notable is Barbie's own coloration; with dark cinnamon skin and black hair, she looks every bit the African goddess. She makes me think of Oshun and Oya.

"Fantasy Goddess of the Americas" (2000) looks like a cross between a kachina, Green Corn Girl, and White Buffalo Calf Woman; a nice blend of different traditions. Her outfit really leans on the "fantasy" side: bare midriff, with a criss-cross top and a split skirt of prominent vertical lines and a gold train. Her massive headdress is a stylized eagle with wings rising above her head and tailfeathers extending down the back. The colors are bright turquoise, dark gold, and white; and the motifs suggest a Southwestern influence. Gold cords fasten her floor-length black braids, a style more typical of the Plains or Eastern nations. My main quibble is that this fair-skinned doll seems to lack the characteristic copper skin tone of Native Americans.

"Fantasy Goddess of the Arctic" (2001) wears a silvery sheath dress with a heavily decorated bodice and a huge swirling cape. Deep blue, her outer garment shows ornate crystalline designs in silver and a thick trimming of white fur all around the borders—unexpectedly lined in brilliant fuscia. Silvery beads dangle from the hood, matching her earrings. A beaded hairband holds up her platinum-blond hair in an intricately twisted crown. Think of Frau Holle, Rind, and Wah-Kah-Nee.

Other Magical Barbies

Along with the Barbies who include "Goddess" in their official names are others with strong magical aspects.

The Celestial Collection presented three dolls in 2000. "Evening Star Princess Barbie" wears a blue gown and veil dusted with glitter; a star crowns her long blond hair. "Midnight Moon Princess Barbie" wears a metallic silver gown and a crown of pearls on her black hair; pearl ropes also connect her bracelets. "Morning Sun Princess Barbie" wears a gold metallic gown and cape, with gold armbands, solar necklace, and sun-ray crown over blond hair. These relate closely to the "Sun Goddess" and "Moon Goddess" Barbies.

"Egyptian Queen Barbie" (1994) belongs to the Great Eras series and wears a blue, gold, and white outfit. Her gold and turquoise headdress suggests royal or priestess status.

The Enchanted Seasons Collection features four dolls. "Snow Princess" (1994), either blond or brunette, wears a white gown trimmed with feathers. "Spring Bouquet" (1995) is blond, in a rainbow dress with a basket of flowers and a sun hat. "Autumn Glory" (1996) is the most magnificent, with auburn hair and shimmering flame-colored dress accented with leaves. "Summer Splendor" (1997) looks adorable in yellow-and-white gingham decorated with daisies and strawberries. Each captures the mood of her quarter, as with seasonal goddesses in many pantheons.

The Enchanted World of Fairies Collection includes two dolls. "Fairy of the Forest" (2000) wears a swirling dress of blue, purple, and green. "Fairy of the Garden" wears a peach dress cut like flower petals. Both have blond hair, filmy wings, and pointed ears that look just like a real fairy's.

The Essence of Nature Collection features three dolls with an elemental theme (earth is omitted, unfortunately). "Water

Rhapsody" (1998) wears a sapphire dress with "wave" train, and a seaspray headpiece over blond hair. "Whispering Wind" (1999) wears a swirly blue and lilac dress and holds a dove in one hand; her blond hair is streaked with blue and lilac. "Dancing Fire" (2000) wears an iridescent orange dress with rising flame-shapes and has red hair.

The Magic & Mystery Collection includes Ken and Barbie as "Merlin" and "Morgan Le Fay" (2000). Dark-haired Morgan wears an outfit of burgundy and gold; snowy-haired Merlin wears a blue robe and carries a gold staff. This may be the most magical Barbie of all!

Finally, from the *Bob Mackie Designer Series* comes "Neptune" (1992), who was originally titled "Neptune's Daughter." Her blue velvet gown, thick with sequins, leaps up around her face, and her platinum hair has a turquoise streak. She stands up well as the sea god's daughter.

Barbie and Paganism

You may be surprised to find Barbie in various manifestations in Pagandom. Most of these are humorous, but some are more serious. It's hard to avoid such a powerful and pervasive cultural icon altogether; sometimes it's better to put your own spin on it.

Possibly the best-known Pagan treatment of Barbie is "The Ancient Goddess Barbie: Historical Views from the Year 5000" by Link. This archeological spoof identifies Barbie as a divine icon based on her prevalence—surmising, for instance, that Ken's lower frequency indicates a matriarchal religion and that the "ancients" made their most important artifacts from long-lasting plastic. It also notes some odd practices in the "contemporary" Barbie cult, such as followers tattooing themselves with the symbols "$24.99." Although written with tongue firmly in cheek, the piece shows a fine grasp of how archaeology and religious reconstructionism work, and how far off our extrapolations may be. The author also touches on some of the aspects that may indeed qualify Barbie as a modern goddess.

There is also a "Barbie Full Moon Ritual" which "honors Barbie, Ken and all things Pink, Blonde, and Plastic." Particularly amusing is the parody of "The Charge of the Goddess," and the representations of the quarters as Pink Feather Boa (East), Pink Hair Dryer (South), Pink Nail Polish (West), and Pink Sand (North). While utterly silly in tone, this piece does remind us of the importance of play. That alone argues well for Barbie's divinity—as long as we can still laugh at ourselves, we can't be too far off-track.

From the ever-growing list of specialty Barbies, it looks like this gal really can be and do anything. Who could resist the temptation to suggest a few more? Cheeky Angel wrote a list of "New Age Barbies" that includes such entries:

> *Gardnerian High Priestess Barbie: Comes complete with ritual robes, headdress, athame, and sterling silver chalice. This one is anatomically correct for skyclad rituals. Altar and High Priest Ken doll sold separately.*

Interestingly, two of the entries parallel actual Mattel items: "Faerie Queen Barbie," who is "complete in green gossamer gown, glowing faerie wand, golden crown, and pointed ears," and "Egyptian Priestess Barbie" who "comes with Isis headdress and ankh, and gown made in the tradition of the 1920's Art Deco Egyptian Look."

Final Thoughts on Barbie

Some people go beyond just making up Barbie names and descriptions. A whole separate branch of Barbie fandom concerns dolls modified by their owners, and the related artwork they create. Consider Dana Lee's "Wiccan Barbie," clad in black dress and stockings, arms upraised in classic priestess pose. She comes with her own athame, wand, and pentacle necklace. "And we've even included a necklace that you can wear, too," says the website, "so you can get into trouble with the principal at your school for wearing Pagan jewellry." Yes, it makes fun of some very serious issues, but sometimes toys and jokes can help us talk about topics otherwise too difficult to bring up.

On a more genuine note, Mamawitch's Pagan Parenting Page features a rite of passage, "Welcoming the Child," intended to honor the end of infancy. It suggests choosing a talisman as a remembrance and as a magical/spiritual tool for the child. The author notes, that her current mantra is "Barbie is an appropriate totem for a girl child." Well, what else would the daughter of a feminist want? Trucks? Don't be silly. Traditionally, dolls and other toys have played an important role in many rites of passage. Given the prominence of Barbie today, this parent's acceptance—however rueful—is likely a better choice than making an unpleasant fuss over the issue.

> Sometimes toys and jokes can help us talk about topics otherwise too difficult or sensitive to bring up.

The practice is neither new nor unique. In an excellent article called "Creatures of Plastic, Creatures of Wax: S/He's a Doll Revisited" by Murtagh A. anDoile and Maire A. ni Morgan explores the historical and contemporary use of dolls in ritual. It describes a ritual wherein a doll represents the Goddess. "Besides the fact that we have used dolls as repositories for energy," they write, "the above ceremony is a compilation of several different rites using a doll (oh my goddess! Barbie . . . by Mattel)."

From a feminist perspective, I find some recent Barbies more palatable than earlier, ditzier models. Some Pagans, however, still object to the whole Barbie concept. They use "Barbie" as a putdown in reference to flaky ideas, goddesses, priestesses, or depictions that they disapprove of. I've heard epithets like "Miss Barbie Witch" and "Barbie Wicca" hurled with considerable venom.

My online research for this article turned up a few phrases like "a ritual robe that would make Barbie blush" and "reducing the Great Goddess to the level of a Barbie doll." From the perspective of someone who tries to encourage civility in the Pagan community, I find such epithets childish and counterproductive. From a linguistic perspective, however, I must admit that they pack crystal-clear meaning.

Not only Pagans note the connections between Barbie and Pagan motifs. Some Barbie scholars have spotted them as well. M. G. Lord, in her book *Forever Barbie,* says there is a remarkable amount of Pagan symbolism surrounding Barbie. "Even the original location of corporate headquarters, Hawthorne, has significance," she writes. "The Hawthorn, or May Tree, represents the White Goddess Maia, the mother of Hermes, goddess of love and death, both the ever-young Virgin giving birth to the God, and the Grandmother bringing him to the end of his season. The cult of the Great Mother was ministered to by eunuchs." Lord further observes that Barbie is both toy and mythic object and a modern woman, "an incarnation of 'The One Goddess with a Thousand Names.'"

So, you may love her or hate her, but it looks like Barbie is here to stay. She is all manner of things to all manner of people, and to some, this doll represents a face of the Goddess. Let us take further encouragement from the fact that a major toy company considers "Goddess" an acceptable word to put on its packaging, and ancient mythology a suitable source of inspiration for contemporary toys and collectibles. Just as pop culture sometimes draws on Pagan inspiration, the reverse can also hold true. Yes, Barbie . . . "Thou, too, art Goddess."

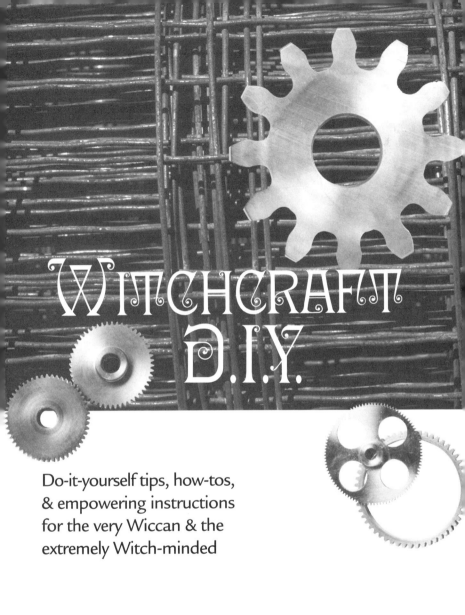

WITCHCRAFT
D.I.Y.

Do-it-yourself tips, how-tos,
& empowering instructions
for the very Wiccan & the
extremely Witch-minded

A Combination Practice: Blending Yoga and Wicca

by Cerridwen Iris Shea

Hello. I am a Witch. I also practice yoga and meditation. In my ideal schedule, I could wander from practice to practice at will, following the whims of my body's bio-rhythms. Unfortunately, there's that pesky necessity of having to work to pay the bills and keep the family fed, clothed, and housed. So I found a way to combine my practices in a way that has strengthened all of them, thereby strengthening me. Here, I share some of my combined practices to provide inspiration for your own fusions.

To start, my altar is placed where I have space. I start the day at the altar, lighting incense and candles. I greet the four directions and my patron deities. Then I do approximately forty minutes of yoga. It's fairly gentle yoga, just simple poses and stretching. It both relaxes and invigorates me.

After the forty minutes of yoga, I sit in the lotus position and follow my breath for a few minutes. I attempt to empty my mind and concentrate on breathing Zen-style. The mind-emptying doesn't always work, but concentrating on counting the breaths often helps. I inhale on odd numbers and exhale on even numbers, doing three sets of ten. I concentrate on letting any negative energy or tension still in the body flow out through my body into the floor and the earth to be recycled into something positive. I fill myself with positive energy, and then sit with that for a few minutes.

I check each chakra, starting at the top of my head and working down. I open each and see if they need work. If so, I take time to pull out the icky stuff (it feels and looks to me like black taffy), and send it into the earth for recycling. I then clean the chakra out with white or pale blue light, and I seal it up.

After the chakra cleansing, I spend a few minutes sending healing or loving energy to anyone in my life who needs it or who has requested it. I consider what needs to be done during the day, and ask for divine guidance and energy to do everything with humor and kindness. I don't always accomplish this, but I try to set that tone for the day. I give thanks for all the wonderful things in my life, ground and center, extinguish the candles (the incense is usually burned out by now), and start my day.

All of this takes about an hour and is well worth getting up early for. My mental and physical health has improved by leaps and bounds since I have used this as my morning devotional. I used to feel continually fatigued and I got sick every few weeks, but now I start my day feeling energized, and I get sick maybe only once or twice a year.

I also like to work with weights to build my strength and stamina. Often, while I do the repetitions I'll repeat the chants of a spell-in-progress. I find it both makes the workout seem faster

and more pleasant, and adds energy to the spell. Sometimes I'll also use chants when I bicycle. Bicycling has a rhythm that complements the chant. One could also chant on a treadmill or stationary bike. I don't use either of those types of machines. It's just me, but I think if I'm going to work that hard I want to end up in a different place than I started!

If I'm in the middle of a long writing day and start feeling fatigued, I often pause in mid-afternoon and allow myself a fifteen- or twenty-minute meditation. Sometimes I use tapes, or else I just light a candle, lie down, and meditate. Pushing yourself when you're running on empty is counterproductive. Usually, a little meditation gives me the jumpstart I need for a few more hours' worth of productive work.

Before I go to sleep at night, I spend a few minutes in front of my altar giving thanks for the day and releasing any stress or negativity I've stored up. If I've had a difficult day, I'll do this as soon as I walk in the door. I try to take a few minutes of calm before I go to sleep, because otherwise my sleep is disturbed. When that happens, I spend more time on the chakra work in the morning. If I've had a physically difficult day, I'll do a few gentle yoga poses, such as the cobra or the knee-and-thigh stretch. I also contemplate my list of blessings for the day. Every night, I give thanks for the myriad small blessings that touched my day.

> I used to feel fatigued and got sick every few weeks, but now I start my day feeling energized, and I get sick maybe once or twice a year.

Each individual has unique needs and rhythms. By combining your physical and contemplative practices, you strengthen both, and this ultimately strengthens your entire body, mind, and spirit.

Mixed Blessings:

Living with a Non-Pagan Partner

by Emely Flak

Like life in general, walking the Pagan path brings interesting challenges and presents us with opportunities to learn. There are times when you will consider disclosing your chosen path to others. With certain people, you may choose to remain silent about your spiritual choice. But what happens when it's your partner who is not Pagan or Wiccan? Eventually, you will want to share this information with that special person in your life. Below are some ideas about ways to manage revealing the truth about yourself to someone you love.

Partners on the Path

Some of us meet our partners when we are already on the path. Others find the path after we are already established in a relationship. Either way, this can be a blessing or a curse depending on the level of understanding and tolerance in your relationship.

Differences in religion, political persuasion, cultural and ethnic background test every relationship, but these are not insurmountable problems. In the cultural potpourri of Western societies, a significant percentage of partner-

> **Differences in religion, political persuasion, cultural and ethnic background test every relationship, but these are not insurmountable.**

ships and marriages are between people of different backgrounds. There is a noticeable increase in marriage ceremonies now officiated by a civil celebrant rather than a minister of religion. This trend suggests that more couples are choosing to exchange vows with a secular ceremony, or else that partners of mixed backgrounds are looking for a celebration that does not focus exclusively on a particular religious path.

When I first spoke of my growing interest in Wicca with my husband, he regarded it as a passing interest. It took some time before he accepted that it was more than a stage I was going through. With your non-Pagan partner, you will probably need first to disclose your Wiccan ways, and afterward you will need to manage the differences in the relationship. There are ways to make a declaration of your Pagan ways easier. With some patience and mutual respect, your relationship of mixed beliefs can be a harmonious and compatible one. Here are some tips to help you manage the process of disclosure.

Don't Assume Immediate Tolerance

When you open discussion about your Pagan ways, your disclosure may not be met with tolerance and understanding. This will depend on your partner's religious upbringing and social conditioning. Although many Western Christians are secular in their

lifestyles and do not attend church regularly, the word "Pagan" or "Witch" will conjure up a strong image in most people's minds. Only after meeting my Pagan friends did my husband realize that his stereotyped idea of Pagans was inaccurate. Instead of meeting a bunch of fringe weirdos, he learned that in fact my friends are balanced and caring people.

Wicca and Paganism are a long way from being accepted as credible religions by most people. You may need to earn respect by behaving ethically and staying true to the path for a period of time. This will also demand patience from you. My husband's initial response is a typical one. But, at the same time, he was able to realize through my commitment to my path that being Pagan did not have negative consequences on my behavior, nor did it change my feelings toward him.

Be Prepared for Questions

Because many people remain skeptical about Paganism and Wicca and perceive it as "alternative" or "occult," expect a range of questions. If your partner's previous exposure to Wicca has been through commercialized Hollywood stuff like Harry Potter, *The Craft,* or *Buffy the Vampire Slayer,* expect to have some explaining to do. Be clear to state that you see Paganism as an ethical spiritual choice. Be prepared to give sound responses to questions, or they may not take you seriously. When in discussion, avoid heated arguments. If you sense strong disagreement, anger, or disbelief creeping into the discussion, explain that you will be happy to discuss the issues when you've both had time to cool down.

Be Respectful of Differences

If you are lucky enough to be with a non-Pagan partner who respects your choice, remember to be equally accepting of his or her non-Pagan ways. This is an important aspect of staying true to your own path—that is, not to judge others by their choices or beliefs. It may be tempting for you to criticize other religions that don't demonstrate the same level of tolerance or respect for nature and gender balance, just for example. Even if your partner is a "secular Christian"—or a Christian who is not particularly religious in practice—remain respectful of this choice. Regard this is an opportunity for you to set a good example and showcase

Paganism and Wicca as having sound ethical frameworks. Be a good ambassador for your path.

Along with being respectful, you may need to consider a compromise. Despite my husband's level of understanding, he prefers that I don't broadcast that fact that I am Wiccan. To accommodate our differences, I walk the Wiccan path quietly rather than with screaming Pagan pride.

I understand his concern. As parent of two school-aged children, my husband worries that other children's parents will misunderstand my choice, and that our children may have to face potential bullying or social isolation. Unfortunately, it's difficult to escape from misinformed people with little understanding of natured-based religions.

For this reason, I am cautious about any making any disclosure outside our close circle of friends. Our two children are being raised in a secular way, with encouragement to find and follow their own spiritual path.

Open Communication

All sound relationships rely on open communication and trust. By all means, talk about what Paganism and Pagan values mean to you. Discuss how you intend to live by those values and how the differences may impact your relationship or home environment. For example, you may need to attend discussion groups or rituals that will not include your partner. You will probably want to create some sacred space in your home for an altar for private ritual and meditation. Let your partner know what takes place at Pagan gatherings. Make your Pagan books and magazines available for them to read, but do not try to force information on them. This unexpectant transparency about the material you read creates a climate of trust and honesty. Avoid a situation where you lead a "double life" away from your partner.

Don't Preach

Resist the temptation to rave on and on about your spiritual passion to the point of annoyance. Your passion may soon become their poison if you overexpose them to endless chatter about your beliefs. Start by assuming they know nothing about the craft, or what they do know may be negative or inaccurate. Be open about the literature you read or receive, but do not expect them to convert themselves just because of your choices. An important aspect of being Wiccan is that you do not preach or try to convert others to your ways. It's a balance of being open about your ways but without excessive discussion that monopolizes all your conversation.

Don't Alienate Your Partner

There is nothing superior about being Pagan or Wiccan. It's an alternative path. It's very possible that despite your efforts to remain open and share your experience without forcing it on your partner, he or she may still see the experience as disconnecting you from your family, friends, or partner. You will need to work hard to reassure that special person in your life that this misunderstood religion is not an evil cult that will lead you astray or take you away.

Change in general makes people feel insecure. Always invite your partner to participate in activities because exclusion can threaten or frighten a partner. I communicate the need to spend time with likeminded people at Pagan and Wiccan discussion groups and conferences, but I always invite my partner to join me. He chooses not to participate but knows that I'm not involved in any "secret activity" because I've offered to include him over and over. If your partner declines your invitation to social gatherings or discussion groups, respect his or her decision without expectations. In a relationship, it is not unusual for couples to maintain separate groups of friends. At least you have demonstrated that you want to share. Avoid condescending remarks like "you wouldn't understand" or "it wouldn't be suitable for you anyway." Emphasize the fact that Wicca and Paganism are tolerant religions that do not claim to be the "only path."

What to Do If They Will Not Accept Your Choice

If your spiritual differences cannot be resolved, like any differences in a relationship you need to firstly ask yourself: Is there a compromise we can make to work this out? I'm not suggesting that all Wiccans should make compromises for their non-Wiccan partners. Rather, ask yourself if a compromise can work in your situation, or if you are prepared to try it out. Also ask: What's best for me—my spiritual choice or my partner? And if you have children, ask: How will any decision you make affect our children? Only you can answer these questions and make the choice. Numerous people have converted their faith to be with the one they love.

Differences are one of many things that challenge and test relationships. Some things we can fully control, others we need to trust that the Goddess is smiling upon us. Luckily, for me, my partner, despite his initial surprise, has remained understanding. I accept that he will never be Pagan or Wiccan, and he accepts that this is my chosen path. It's been a lesson that has helped us grow together as we've learned about tolerance, human diversity, and unconditional love. Relationships like these that are treated with respect and open communication can prove to be a mixed blessing.

Creative Recycling for a Modern Pagan Lifestyle

by Ruby Lavender

We all know it's good to recycle for various reasons. Recycling helps the environment by reducing the waste that goes to landfill. It saves us money by allowing us to consume less and reuse more, and it allows us to find creative ways of reusing items and avoiding the constant necessity (or temptation) of buying new ones.

Pagans are especially interested in recycling, I have found, but this is for reasons that go beyond environmental awareness and saving money. Pagans also like to reuse things because they often have a special appreciation for older items and older designs. They also appreciate the creative utilization of objects, and finding interesting uses for things. And finally, on a spiritual level they often align themselves with earlier cultures that tended to be more conservative and careful when it came to utilizing resources.

Native Americans cultures, for example, were in general oriented to avoid doing anything that radically altered the landscape where they lived. To many tribal cultures, the land was sacred. Living upon it was something that required care and forethought. Digging a well is not as simple as making a hole to draw water from. One must consider how such a project would affect other aspects of the landscape. Further, tribal peoples of old would try to use every single part of animal they'd hunted: the flesh and organs for food; the hide for clothing; the brains for tanning the hide; the tail, horns, claws, teeth, and so on for weapons, tools, or costume ornament.

Pagans are especially interested in recycling. They often have an appreciation for older items and older designs.

These days, we buy prepared foods in elaborate packaging that we throw away instantly. We think "disposable" is a good thing, never thinking that the more we dispose of, the more we add to the solid waste problem. If Pagans wish to return to a way of life that honors the Earth, then we must be very aware of the often careless and excessive use of resources that has become so common in modern society. Of course it is not practical for some of us to hunt for our meat or grow our own vegetables or make our own clothes, but we can make a difference by being thoughtful about how much we consume and by finding creative ways to make the most of what we have.

This article cannot address every single aspect of recycling and living simpler, but I do want to at least mention some issues common to many urban Pagans and to offer suggestions for lessening your personal consumption and waste. I will primarily address items purchased and used for ritual or magical activities and Pagan gatherings.

Candle Recycling Tips

Since I have never met a Pagan who did not use candles for some purpose, let's start there. Candles are wonderful; they are usually inexpensive, yet they create a soft glow to illuminate a room, keep insects away, and waste little energy. However, once candles burn down, there are those empty containers to worry about. That is, many of us buy candles in containers that the candles have been poured into. Do we just toss these after we're done with the candle?

Actually, there are several ways to reuse these containers. First, you can put more candles in them! To do this you don't need any special equipment, although you may want to familiarize yourself with basic candlemaking instructions, including safety tips, from a craft book or website. You'll need candle wicks, which are available at crafts shops and hobby supply stores. You can buy new wax (paraffin mixed with beeswax is a great combination; the beeswax has a higher melting point but makes the candle last longer and smells great), or you can reuse wax drippings from used candles. If you're really organized, you can put similarly colored or scented candles together. If you are recycling unscented candles, you can add a few drops of essential oils to scent them. Some inexpensive essential oils that will offer wonderful aromatherapy benefits are: lavender (cleansing and relaxing), lemon (refreshing and cleansing), patchouli (sensual and earthy), grapefruit (energizing), and clove (spicy and warming).

Making the candles is straightforward but somewhat tricky. Be sure to remove all bits of metal, wick, or other material from the used wax before melting it. Put the wax in a double boiler (a clean coffee can in a saucepan of water works) to melt it.

Once you have melted the wax and are ready to put it into the jar, suspend a candle wick over the top of a jar by tying it to a pencil. Hold the pencil still with the wick hanging straight down to the bottom of the jar. Pour the melted wax carefully into the jar up to the desired height. Let it cool and then harden for a

day or two in a cool place, and you have a brand new candle!

You can in fact pour your own candles into any other sort of container you want to recycle as long as it is made of material that can take heat. To be safe, glass is your best bet. Be sure to review basic candlemaking instructions for safety, and never pour wax down the drain.

Another use for those old candle jars is as flower vases. I like to reuse the "saint" candles for this purpose because many of them are colorful and beautiful. To do this, just rinse out the jars. Do not worry if a bit of wax remains in the bottom. You can even choose particular saints that correspond with particular flowers to help enhance a spell or to add some special magical energy to an occasion or ritual. (Check out any of the many magical encyclopedias for these correspondences). The jars can also be used to store pens and pencils, loose incense sticks, long fireplace matches, or, you guessed it, taper-shaped candles!

I also recycle candle wax by using it while camping at Pagan gatherings. I add it to the campfire as a source of fuel or as a nice firestarter. It is actually much better than the stinky and toxic chemical starters. Melted wax can be poured out of candles into a sluggish fire that has burned down or that has been built with damp wood. Do be extremely careful when doing this. Some people will toss the melted wax on top of a lit candle or "bug bucket" into a campfire without thinking, and the resulting flare-up can be very dangerous! (I almost had my entire head of hair burned off by a very careless person who did this a few years ago without warning anyone what she was about to do). Make sure no one is near the fire, announce what you are about to do, and *never* put in more than a very small amount at one time.

Camp Recycling Tips

Another trick for campfires when at gatherings is to recycle your trash for use in firestarting. Using paper plates, cups, and bowls saves on water resources and cuts down on trash, plus it makes an excellent nontoxic way to start your campfire easily. Just make sure no plastic utensils or foil are mixed in; these give off toxic fumes when burned.

Some Pagans throw their cigarette butts into the fires. I tend to think this is a bad idea, because the toxic smoke that results from the chemicals in the filters is every bit as harmful as smoking is. Still, when camping disposing of butts is a problem. I personally think smokers should be in charge of finding the best disposal method. Most campers know to "field-strip" their cigarettes when finished—that is, to shred the remaining paper and tobacco into the fire and then to pocket or dispose of the filter somewhere else. One should also take such care when out walking on trails where no waste disposal can is nearby.

Herbs are also used by many Pagans for spellwork and incense. But after a while, some herbs lose their potency of fragrance or color, so we may no longer wish to use them for magical workings. Still, they should not be thrown away.

Dried herbs make a lovely and fragrant addition to a campfire. You can sprinkle certain herbs over your charcoal when grilling to add flavor and fragrance—though only herbs, and not resins, should be used for this. Rosemary makes a terrific herbal incense and a great herb for the grill fire; it is particularly good with savory meats like pork or lamb. Lavender is also a nice; try it for fish. Dried patchouli might make for an interesting flavor, but I have not tried it myself. My tip is that you should experiment with small quantities. Most powdered woods used for making incense do not ever lose their fragrance, but if you wish to recy-

cle them because they are of a certain age, they are also nice additions to the fire.

Cedar, sandalwood, and vetiver might be too strong for adding to cooking fires but are wonderful for campfires. Cherry, oak, willow, and hazel are used by many Witches for magical purposes and would be perfect for cooking fires.

Tips for Herbs and Essential Oils

While we are on the subject of recycling, know that part of the reason to reduce and reuse has to do with the rarity or availability of substances. Sandalwood, for example, is now becoming increasingly endangered because the trees are being used up rapidly for the cosmetics and fragrance industry. Sandalwood essential oil is best harvested from trees thirty years old or older, but the demand has grown too great for harvesters to wait that long. So do everyone a favor and limit your use of precious plant materials. Sandalwood, rosewood, frankincense, and myrrh are all less plentiful (and accordingly more expensive) than they used to be. Experiment with alternatives for your incense-making. Copal, benzoin, and dragon's blood resin are all excellent for incense and none of them are from endangered sources (at least not yet).

Speaking of herbs, the storage of herbs is always a concern. Should they be kept in the paper or plastic bags they are purchased in? Do I need a separate shelf or cabinet? Well, although the answers will depend upon your own needs, generally-speaking herbs should be stored in glass jars.

Plastics contain chemicals that can "migrate" into other materials under certain conditions (exposure to heat, for example). Herbs therefore should also be kept in a cool, dry environment away from sunlight, bright light, or any extremes in temperature. A separate shelf or cabinet is always a nice thing if you can arrange it, especially if you have a large selection of herbs. But the main point I want to make here is that there is no need for special containers. I have seen Pagans and Witches who organize their herb supply in jars of Spanish glass, corked and arranged on an antique spice rack, and this is overkill, plain and simple. You can recycle glass containers with lids and create your own "custom" collection. Simply take care to avoid lids that retain strong odors; this can be true of some seasonings (like garlic powder) or foods (like spaghetti sauce). In these cases, soaking the lids in water with either white vinegar or baking soda might help.

Store herbs in clean containers that are appropriate to the amount you tend to keep on hand. If some herbs are tricky to pour, store them in jars with smaller openings. Labels are helpful. You can print your own on your computer, or hand-letter them on paper and use invisible tape to attach them to jars. Some people keep their medicinal herbs in one spot, their magical ones somewhere else, and their incense resins in still another place. Just be sure to keep the area as clean as possible so dust does not get mixed in with your herbs.

You can also reuse glass jars to store oils you've made. Be aware that essential oils can break down plastic, so your glass jars should have metal lids. For safety, handle bath oils and salts in glass jars extremely carefully; measure amounts out into a plastic cup before putting them into the bath. Having broken glass on a porcelain tub surface is very dangerous. Those Pagans who work with

There is no need for special herb containers. Some organize their herb supply in jars of Spanish glass, corked, and arranged on an antique spice rack. This is overkill.

perfumery or aromatherapy may be familiar with the frustration of essential oils losing their efficacy. This does not tend to happen when they are properly stored, and many essential oils, such as those from woods or resins like vetiver and sandalwood, actually improve with age. But some of the lighter florals are more delicate in composition and inevitably do change in time. Still, don't thrown them away. Use them in the rinse water of your handwashing, or in the final rinse after shampooing. You can also add them to shampoos, conditioners, or body lotions for added fragrance, just be sure to check first whether they are known to be skin irritants. Some of the citrus oils can cause a bit of photosensitivity in skin products, for example, but you won't generally use enough to worry about this. Peppermint can cause slight burning in mucous membranes. Clove, cinnamon, and ginger essential oils should not be used in skin products.

General Thrift

I have one rather obvious suggestion that can help the savvy Pagan reduce, reuse, and recycle: shop at thrift stores! I have been doing this for many years and cannot even tell you some of the amazing Pagan treasures I have found at the Goodwill, Salvation Army, and similar types of places. Just to name a few, I've found vintage smoking jackets, silver goblets, fancy antique candlesticks, and a carving set made of sterling silver and deer antlers that were carved to look like a boar's head ringed with oak leaves and acorns.

If you look carefully, you can find very inexpensive items and clothing suitable for use in ritual. Check the sections with long gowns and sleepwear for some interesting ritual robe possibilities. Vintage leathers can be cut up for various crafts like scabbards, moccasins, or other costume pieces. Check the kitchenwares for athames, chalices, candleholders, and similar items. Hunting through housewares can yield linens to be used for altar cloths (or for the ambitious, refashioned into robes), statuary, or wall art for your temple.

By reusing something another person has discarded, you send a message that you are not contributing to the "throwaway mentality" that seems so prevalent today. You are also bestowing value upon an item that was left unloved. If you feel a need to cleanse an item of any potential negative energy before using it magically, water, salt, earth or air are all acceptable materials for this, as are any simple spells of banishing or cleansing.

Finally, I have a suggestion for getting rid of items you no longer need or want: have a swap! Clothing and books make excellent swap items, and this is a nice change of pace from the usual rummage sale. Contact a bunch of your Pagan friends, and invite them to bring their unwanted books or clothes. Tell them this is a swap, and they should bring things other people will likely want. Have a potluck, or have everyone chip in and order a pizza.

At the actual swap, everyone is allowed to exchange one of their items for one someone else has brought. This can be organized any number of ways; the easiest is to get a count of someone's donated items and count how many they want to take with them. Anything left over can be donated to local charities or put away for a future swap.

Over time you may decide you could have a ritual item swap with fellow practitioners. Once you begin to consider the many ways there are of creatively reducing, reusing, and recycling, the possibilities may seem endless.

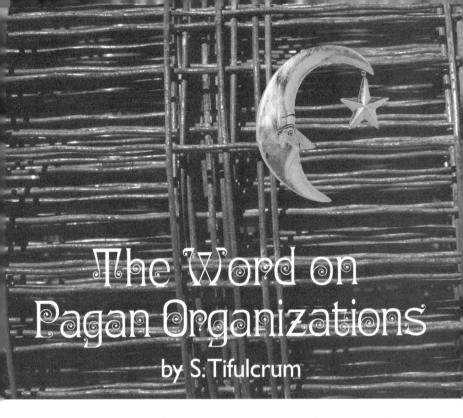

The Word on Pagan Organizations

by S. Tifulcrum

Whether you're a new seeker or a well-seasoned elder, you probably know that one thing many Wiccans yearn for is a sense of community. Sure, there are e-mail lists and web groups for just about everything under the Sun, but what if all you want is to find a nice group of people with similar interests and professions who just happen to be Pagan? Is it a hopeless cause?

Fear not! You may be surprised to know that there are indeed a number of Pagan organizations dedicated to various activities, interests, and careers. It's easy enough to type a few keywords into a search engine and locate some of these, but for those of you who prefer to do your seeking offline, this is the place for you! What follows are some of the more visible (as well as up and coming) organizations that might just become your new Pagan "family."

How to Begin Finding Pagan Organizations

To begin with, it seemed the best way to approach all these organizations would be to lump them together into categories with headings that explain the primary function of each group.

You may be surprised to know that there are a number of Pagan organizations dedicated to various activities, interests, and careers. While this is hardly an exact science, and this listing is in no way intended to be comprehensive, it appeared that four main headings could be applied to most of these sorts of groups: professional organizations, educational organizations, activist and support organizations, and miscellaneous organizations.

Many of the groups mentioned in this article actually could fit into two or more of these headings. Rather than try to cross-reference everything, groups have been placed according to their primary intent. That is, if a given group does a lot of educational work but is also involved to a lesser degree in political activism, that group will be listed as educational. Multiple goals are noted in the description of the group where appropriate.

Professional Pagan Organizations

This category covers organizations that focus on one or more related professions. Members are typically Pagan, but not necessarily of one specific path, and have worked in, or are interested in, a profession. Individuals meet to share ideas, network, gain knowledge, and in some cases, get specialized training—all with like-minded people who share the Pagan's unique perspective.

Since in many cases it is difficult to be out of the broom closet in a workplace environment, this can be a particularly valuable resource for many.

PAGAN ☆ ORGANIZATIONS

professional

educational

activist & support

miscellaneous

Military Pagan Network (MPN)

Pagans in the military can turn to the Military Pagan Network for assistance in dealing with religious discrimination and harassment issues. In addition, the MPN reviews and proposes changes to military regulations to take into account the practices of Pagans serving in uniform. The MPN is tax-exempt under section 501(a) of the Internal Revenue Code as an organization described in section 501(c)3, and has a $10 membership fee. To join, you must submit a military ID card or a DD214 to verify your military status. For more info, see: http://www.milPagan.org/.

Officers of Avalon

Formed in 1999, the Officers of Avalon is an international organization of Pagans with law enforcement backgrounds as correctional officers, military, and other emergency responders such as firefighters, paramedics, and emergency medical technicians. The bulk of the membership is from the U.S. and Canada. The spokesperson for this group is the well-known author and Canadian police officer Kerr Cuhulain, who has written the books *The Law Enforcement Guide to Wicca, Full Contact Magick,* and *Wiccan Warrior.* See: http://www.officersofavalon.org/.

Pagan Bar Association

The Pagan Bar Association is a social community that requires members to be lawyers in good standing with their state or provincial bar associations, or students in good standing enrolled in an accredited law school program. There are no dues or other fees involved with membership. For more information, contact Angeleno at greifen2000@yahoo.com with "PBA Inquiry" in the subject line of your email.

Pagan Internet Designers & Developers Association (PaganIDEA)

With an international membership hailing from Australia to Canada and beyond, PaganIDEA is a community of web designers, graphic artists, and computer programmers who also happen to be Pagan. The group shares information, ideas, and experience, as well as providing training for members who wish to improve their skills. PaganIDEA was established in 2001, and has plans to obtain legal nonprofit status. There are no fees or restrictions on membership. For more info, see: http://www.Paganidea.org/.

Pagan Schoolteachers

This is primarily a network for Pagan teachers. Members exchange support and information about how Pagans are received in various school districts where members may work. Job openings are sometimes posted to the list, and advice is shared on various topics. Membership is open, and there are no fees or dues. See: http://groups.yahoo.com/group/Paganteachers/.

Educational Organizations

This is the most common category, and something of a catch-all. Pagans tend to be a brainy bunch, so it's not surprising that virtually all of the organizations mentioned have an educational component to them. The main function of educational organizations is to provide education to the public and training to group members, and to develop educational resources. This may include hosting workshops, presenting at fairs and conferences, writing articles for publication, conducting ongoing research, and offering training opportunities.

Alternative Religions Educational Network (AREN)

AREN has undergone quite a transformation since its inception nearly thirty years ago. At that time, it was called the Witches Anti Defamation League (WADL), though the name soon changed to a "Lobby," rather than a league. In 1996, WADL was changed back to "League," and the group's fight against religious discrimination continued. WADL changed its name again in the year 2000 to become the Alternative Religions Educational Network (AREN). According to their website, AREN hopes to go out of business eventually—once there is a lack of discriminatory cases for it to fight. The organization is incorporated as an educational support group, though it is highly activist in fulfilling these functions. Membership is $15/year in the U.S., and $30/year elsewhere. For more info, see: http://www.aren.org/.

Pagan Educational Network (PEN)

Founded in 1993 and incorporated in 1997, PEN focuses on providing education to the public as well as creative solutions to problems facing Pagan communities. Specific issues of interest are protecting Pagans' constitutional rights, and building community through service. The group does not use war language (such as "fighting for rights") and requires all of its published material to clearly demonstrate how readers can use the information in daily life. PEN is an American nonprofit, proactive group with membership fees on a sliding scale. See: http://www. bloomington.in.us/~pen/.

PagaNet, Inc. (PNI)

PNI is a legally incorporated organization whose primary mission is to provide professional and sustainable support to the earth-based religious community. The group is entirely volunteer and provides a variety of services including religious and leadership education, public lectures and presentations, and social programs and activities. In addition, PNI is working toward ownership of sixty-plus acres of land in Virginia for use as a spiritual retreat resource center for Pagans. Presently there are no membership dues, but plans were underway at the time of this writing to create a membership base which would include dues to cover organizational costs. Some PNI events may require a registration fee. See: http://www.Paganet.org/.

Witches' League for Public Awareness (WLPA)

While many organizations exist to educate the public about Witches and witchcraft, the WLPA also works to correct the misinformation that already exists. It is a proactive educational network that was founded in 1986 by the well-known author Laurie Cabot. The WLPA is also interested in getting Pagans to become registered voters and to express their political opinions through voting. The WLPA has yearly membership dues based on category of membership. See: http://www.celticcrow.com/.

Activist and Support Organizations

The organizations listed here are either openly activist in nature, or dedicated to providing support services to Pagans. Some of the groups are actually more educational in nature, but activism or support plays such an important role in the make-up of the group that it seemed best to place them here instead. There is no

My list is intended to be a starting point for your own research. You'll find many other groups that suit your own needs.

distinction made at this level between those groups that are for-profit or nonprofit, save to say that nonprofit groups cannot participate in political lobbying, whereas for-profit groups may do so. Other differences exist, but for our purposes they are relatively minor.

Lady Liberty League (LLL)

The Lady Liberty League (LLL) is the religious freedom branch of the international Wiccan church and resource center, Circle Sanctuary. In 1978, Circle incorporated as a Wiccan church in Wisconsin and received federal recognition two years later. The LLL was born in 1985, and since then has provided information and assistance to those concerned with religious freedom issues not only concerning Wiccans, but also other forms of nature religion. The LLL is entirely volunteer and has specialists covering a wide range of legal, military, and child custody issues. For more info, see: http://www.circlesanctuary.org/liberty/.

Pagan Aid Network (PAN)

The Pagan Aid Network is a nonprofit humanitarian organization currently being formed to coordinate and assist volunteers who wish to help victims of disasters. PAN will also attempt to provide emergency food and housing assistance in hardship situations. In cases where the group is unable to help, they will try to refer victims to the proper agencies. See: http://www.Pagan-aid.org.

Pagan Unity Campaign (PUC)

The PUC's stated mission is to unify the diverse branches of Paganism in America under the banner of freedom. There is no formalized membership, as the PUC is entirely a volunteer organization. Volunteers have taken action on various events, such as the "I am" letter-writing campaign to notify politicians of the number of Pagan voters in America. The PUC is also active in getting Pagans to register to vote and to actually hit the polls on election days. See: http://www.Paganunitycampaign.org/.

Witches Against Religious Discrimination (WARD)

WARD has been around since the late 1990s and is active in various areas such as prison ministry, media monitoring, and providing investigative and legal support in discrimination cases. Divisions include a child safety branch as well as fundraising, education, and research. Membership options range from a free membership to a $60 membership, with perks varying according to level. See: http://www.ward-hq.org/.

Miscellaneous Organizations

The last category is diverse in its composition. Some groups included here are large church-like organizations that have a designated function aside from being an avenue for religious worship or gatherings. The Sacred Well Congregation of Texas is a good example of this. Although the SWC is a legally recognized church with a specific Wiccan tradition, it is also heavily involved in supporting military Pagans who wish to practice their faith while in uniform. Other organizations listed under this category include resource centers that are communities as well.

Covenant of the Goddess (CoG)

One of the largest and oldest Wiccan organizations, the Covenant of the Goddess (CoG) is an umbrella organization that allows individual groups to confer legally recognized clergy credentials upon members who meet certain requirements. Members may also be granted clergy credentials independent of any other group. Solitaries are welcome as part of the Assembly of Solitaries. Other CoG activities include youth scholarship awards, counseling, sponsorship of campus and youth groups, and legal assistance in discrimination cases. The Covenant of the Goddess obtained status as a nonprofit religious organization after its incorporation on October 31, 1975. Membership requires sponsoring by current CoG members. More information can be found on their webpage: http://www.cog.org.

Deaf Pagan Resource Center
A unique group that strives to be a resource for Pagans who are deaf, hard of hearing, or are simply interested in this community. Educational materials include articles on how deaf Pagans celebrate rituals, how to raise deaf Pagan children, and how to set up a networking community. There is no membership as such, but there are regular e-list members who comprise the core of the Deaf Pagan Resource Center. See: http://www.deafPagan.org/.

Goddess Moon Circles (GMC)
This organization is difficult to classify owing to the sheer amount of services it provides. Education and community service is paramount, with Pagan pantries, food and clothing drives, and much more on their website. Goddess Moon also lists Pagan clergy and alternative medicine resources, pastoral and spiritual counseling resources (crisis counseling also available), and a Pagan-oriented homeschooling program—Goddess Moon Circles Academy—for preschool through senior high school. A three-year clergy ordination program is also available through GMC. Check out the site for much more information, including arts and crafts, domestic abuse assistance, and pregnancy and childbirth resources: http://www.goddessmoon.org.

Sacred Well Congregation (SWC)
The SWC is a universalist, independent Wiccan church that was incorporated in Texas in 1996. It follows the Greencraft Tradition

and has as its primary missions education and the provision of open, public venues for the safe practice of alternative religions. As a direct result, the SWC is heavily involved in sponsoring military Pagan groups worldwide. The SWC is also leading the way towards gaining authority to nominate Wiccan chaplains for possible military service. A clergy ordination program is also available through the SWC, although it follows a traditional degree format. There are seven levels of membership, ranging from general membership to commercial supporting organizational membership. Dues are based on category, although general membership does not require any dues—just a $10 donation requested to help defray organizational costs. For more info, see: http://www.sacredwell.org.

Your Own Research

My list is only intended to be a starting point for your own research. You'll find many other groups that suit to your particular needs and interests. In fact, you might even find there are a few in your local area for more hands-on participation than cyberspace allows. Best of luck to you in your search.

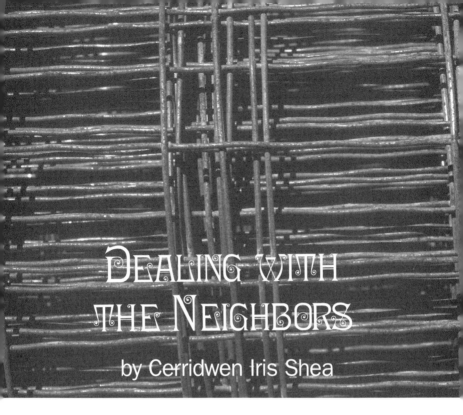

Dealing with the Neighbors

by Cerridwen Iris Shea

Unless you live the fairy-tale life of yore, with a Witch's cottage in the woods and woodland creatures singing at your window, sooner or later you have to deal with the neighbors. And chances are, the neighbors will follow a different religious path than you do. In fact, chances are some of them would just as soon run away screaming as live next door to you. But rest assured, there are ways to achieve peaceful coexistence in most situations, no matter if you are the newcomer to the neighborhood or are already established and welcoming new neighbors yourself.

Tips for Getting Along with the Neighbors

To start off, it's good policy not to lead off any new relationship by revealing your religion. That's not being hypocritical. It's letting your neighbors get to know you as a human being before any other factor. Saying, "Hi, I'm Cerridwen. I live next door. Let me know if there's anything I can do to help you get settled," will be just fine. You might bring some cookies or flowers with you as well. Usually, when new neighbors move in, I give them a list with directions to grocery stores, cleaners, newsstand, and whatever else might be helpful—especially if they don't know the town.

On the flip side, when I'm the one moving in, I don't wait for the neighbors to come by and introduce themselves. I bake cookies and leave bags of them at their doors with a note introducing myself. You don't have to become best friends with them just because they live next door, but treating them with kindness will go a long way to establishing a good neighborly relationship.

Actions always speak louder than words. I decorate my home to celebrate the seasons. My door often looks like a craft fair truck crashed into it. But the neighbors like it and offer me compliments. Several say they look forward to the turn of the season because they can't wait to see what I'll come up with next.

I have altars and shrines in prominent positions in the home, and I don't try to hide them when someone rings the doorbell. I work to keep a positive environment by doing my smudgings and cleansings regularly. My home reflects not only my spirituality, but also my love of animals (four friendly, bossy cats), my interest in sports, quilting, cooking, travel, literature, and the fact that I'm a writer and tarot card reader. There's a sense of fun and peace in the space, after all it is my sanctuary. When people walk through the front door, they usually immediately relax and exclaim at how great the space feels.

As people get to know me and ask me questions, I answer simply and honestly. I don't get into long, involved explanations. I try always to be a good neighbor. Consideration is key here.

There are times when loud chanting outside at midnight during a Full Moon circle is not fair to the neighbors. Living in a densely populated neighborhood, we often have our circles inside, and maybe have our feast outside.

Some other tips to be more neighborly: Try taking your neighbors' packages in, helping them shovel snow, or giving them a jumpstart when the car battery dies. When the neighborhood kids sell candy to raise money for a school trip, go ahead and buy something. Say good morning, good evening, and hello when passing a neighbor. Take the five extra minutes to have a conversation. Use compassion. Instead of getting mad at the neighbor trying to strap her screaming child into the car seat as the car stands in the driveway, walk over and help her out. Send healing energy out first in times of difficulty. Live a path of tolerance, joy, and kindness.

Try getting involved in your neighborhood. When you move to a new place, change your voter's registration. Find out the recycling policies in your area; visit your neighborhood organization. Be conscientious with everyone, and learn all that you can about your neighbors and neighborhood. Show that you're interested in what happens there, and that you are a positive force in the community.

What to Do in the Worst Case

Sometimes, despite your best efforts, there may be times when your neighbors are so disturbed and frightened by your beliefs that no peaceful coexistence is possible. In that case, it is important not to roll over and accept the way it is. Keep a log of any vandalism, or verbal or physical abuse. File complaints with the police department. E-mail the incident to people you can trust; ask them to print it out and keep a file for you. Take photographs, make audiotapes—you are protected by the legal system. If you have to move, then plan to do so.

If things get rough, try using invisibility and glamoury spells. Before you move to a new area, take the time to find out if

it is a place you feel you could not only survive, but thrive. In the current economy, we often feel we have to accept any job offer in order to survive. But mental health is just as important. Try some ritual and magic to find out where you're supposed to be. We live our path and make our magic to improve our own corner of the world. Being a good neighbor is a part of that. Be positive, truthful, and kind, and it will create bonds through barriers.

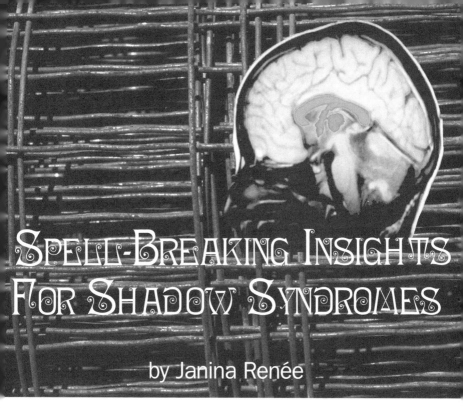

Spell-Breaking Insights
For Shadow Syndromes

by Janina Renée

Thanks to the "new" neurology, we are learning about ways that brain chemicals and structure are involved in a number of major mental disorders such as full-blown autism, bipolar disorder, obsessive-compulsive disorder, Tourette's syndrome, and in other "shadow syndromes." These are cases where a person may have only some parts of a mental illness that, if he or she suffered from the full-blown syndrome, would be unmistakable.

A person with a shadow syndrome may have a number of minor symptoms that are associated with several different mental disorders. Or he or she may suffer just a few mild symptoms characteristic of one particular disorder, or all the symptoms of a particular disorder but in a very mild form. Because shadow syndromes can be low-key, they often escape diagnosis. Still, their symptoms can have a sharp effect on the lives of individuals, locking them into stereotypical personality types, messing with their perception of reality, and affecting their ability to find suitable employment and maintain relationships with other people. As this shadow population is well represented in the magical community, our knowledge of these syndromes has some major implications.

For instance, these syndromes contribute to "Cognitive Otherness"—a different way of perceiving, experiencing, and acting upon the world. Persons with Cognitive Otherness are more likely drawn to metaphysical systems and to the margins of society. Some autistic people see a glow or vibration around the edges of people and things. Some might dismiss such phenomena as neurological distortions, but it may also be that such neurological quirks promote supernormal perceptive abilities.

It is entirely possible that some of the history and lore of magic may have been observations of persons with shadow syndromes. I long ago read that the English accused Anne Boleyn, the second wife of King Henry VIII, of being a Witch because she couldn't look people in the eyes. She also was so sensitive to sound that she silenced all the church bells in her area. Another example: prevalent among the eastern and southern Slavs is the belief that if you are being chased by a Witch or vampire, you should scatter a handful of straw or lentils on the floor, as the Witch or vampire will be forced to count them while you escape. Counting is an obsessive-compulsive, and sometimes an autistic, trait. Also, the belief that vampires can't enter a room unless invited reminds me of Asperger's syndrome, wherein people can't make certain moves unless permission is spelled out. If more were known about persons accused of being sorcerers, possessors of the evil eye, and so on, I imagine we would find a large number of shadow syndrome sufferers—people who tried to pass for normal but whose weirdness inevitably revealed itself.

At the same time, I believe that shadow syndrome people are more prone to maladies that are well-known to folk practitioners, but have no equivalent in modern medicine—such as *susto* and *espanto* (shock-related soul loss) and *bilis* (rage disorder and emotional upset).

In general, metaphors of the supernatural are helpful in understanding some of the problems associated with shadow syndromes. Take the issue of embodiment—how a person lives in his or her body can be affected by these disorders. From my own misadventures as a person with Asperger's syndrome—experiencing delays and distortions in sensory processing, perpetually being out of synch with other people, constant mental static, petite trances, clumsiness, inability to multitask—I've come to describe it as a case of spirit possession.

There are magical implications in *naming* a disorder, as knowing the name of a thing can give you power over it and can effect transformation. The old Norse had a belief in werewolves and *maras*—women who left their bodies and gave other people nightmares. If you saw someone while he or she was in werewolf or mara form and you said his or her name aloud, the spell would be broken and the person returned to human. Likewise, if you encountered such persons in human form and pointed out that they were a werewolf or mara, that would also lift the spell.

When I was young, the diagnosis of Asperger's syndrome was not available. When I learned about it later in life, after my son was diagnosed, this did not magically make the syndrome go away, but it explained all kinds of my quirky behaviors that never made sense, and also helped me form strategies for managing them.

Since becoming attuned to my syndrome's traits, I've made others aware of their own Asperger's symptoms, and I try to be

frank in telling depressed friends they are depressed, and so on. Shadow syndrome people go through their lives knowing that something is wrong, but they don't have a name for it. And having a name for what ails you is the first step in coping.

Drawing from metaphysical theories and folk magic practices, we can bring magical awareness to some of these problems. For example, according to the theories of Jeffrey Schwartz, obsessive-compulsive symptoms are caused by brain-lock due to a malfunction of three brain sections: the caudate nucleus, which effects the flow of thought, and, in normal people, has a "gating mechanism" for suppressing distracting thoughts; the orbital cortex, which houses the brain's "error-detection circuit"; and the cingulate gyrus, which is responsible for the severe psychic pain of obsessive-compulsive disorder.

If I were to compose a spell for a mildly obsessive-compulsive type of person known as a "social scanner," that is, someone who experiences mental anguish from endlessly going over his or her social faux pas, I would personify this troublesome tendency by creating entities through the following traditional charm format. In a short version, the entities encounter a divine being—a manifestation of the god Mercury, messenger of the gods. The charm reads: "As the Gracious One trod a winding road, he met three women by an open gate. 'Ladies, you must do right by [your name here]. The ladies consent and close the gate, and you feel peace and comfort."

The long version of this charm brings in elements of Sephardic *prekantes* (lengthy curing rituals) by describing what the ladies look like, and what they say and do (using more symbolic brain imagery). Recite this spell first thing in the morning or whenever the bothersome thoughts start repeating, or else write it down, or have others say it to you as part of a ritual. After reading or writing the verse, you should immediately turn your attention to any wholesome, diverting activity, as a way of training the brain to fully let go of the obsessive issues.

A means of dealing with some of the more harmless symptoms of certain syndromes is to try exaggerating them in a controlled context, and see where that takes you. For example, some autistics engage in twirling motions, similar to what whirling dervishes do in ritual. I believe that rocking behavior has a brain-integrative function, so instead of feeling ashamed of it, I use a stepped-up rocking motion to help with inspiration when writing. It's interesting to note that sometimes Jewish religious scholars use a similar motion when reading sacred texts.

You can also use amuletic objects, such as a piece of brain coral on a home altar as a symbol of good brain functioning and mindfulness. Or you might contemplate the wavy, variegated

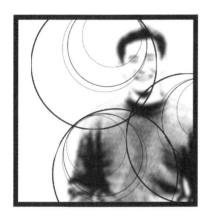

lines of an agate as a way of calming the mind and restoring focus. If you can put a name on certain conditions, symptoms, or behaviors that bother you, you could inscribe them on a candle and let it burn through them, or else try the Hoodoo technique of inscribing them on a bar of soap and throwing it into a river. If you are able to make anagrams out of these conditions, even if they form nonsense words or phrases, you can recite or inscribe a string of the anagrams as a way of putting the behaviors in their place and making them look ridiculous. But set a limit, because anagramming can be an obsessive pursuit.

Names can also serve as "words of power." Thus, one can recite the magical names of Bill Gates, Albert Einstein, Thomas Jefferson, Charlotte Perkins Gilman, Rainer Maria Rilke, and others to people who are skeptical or worried about the stigma of shadow syndromes.

It is not within the scope of this article to go into greater depth, but creative ritualists will see the possibilities for further exploration. Remember that we are talking about *mild* disorders here, and that persons with more serious problems should seek appropriate medical care. Also, I am not suggesting that any of these countermagic techniques can "cure" the shadow syndrome, merely that they can help make certain conditions visible and tangible in a way that makes it easier to contain them.

Sweep Me Away!

Tips & suggestions
for Wiccans who wander
through the wide &
wondrous world

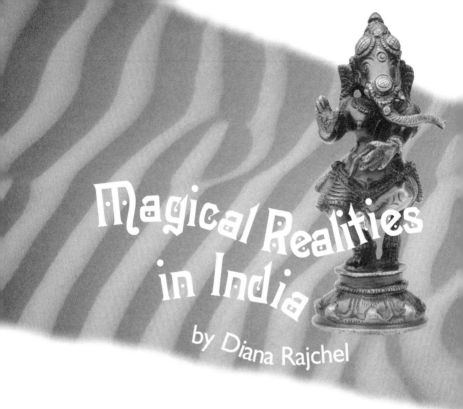

Magical Realities in India

by Diana Rajchel

One of the most often misunderstood
differences between Eastern and Western
cultures concerns the delineation of the
"real" and the "not real." Westerners, for
example, still deny the existence of Witches
or confuse such individuals with legendary
and folkloric figures, while Easterners
accept Witches as a reality of modern life.
Eastern people in fact view these people as
providers of services just as necessary to
their lives as a plumber or a doctor.

While certainly not at the forefront of
society in India, Witches do assume a role
in society. While police officers and teachers
are often described as the "first line of

defense" in India, Witches serve as the last line of defense in addressing issues that fall outside of everyday control. When families experience troubles with illness, unemployment, long streaks of bad luck, nightmares, or other unexplained phenomena, they naturally first apply for help from doctors, healers, and priests. If these professionals fail to correct the problems, then a Witch is sought for assistance. The services that families request of Witches ranges from exorcism to curses. For a few rupees, Witches will take on the requests.

Roots of Traditional Witchcraft in India

The Witches of India are associated with a tradition of Hinduism known as tantra. It is not clear whether all Witches are tantrics, but it is believed that their power is acquired through tantric practices. Hindus of other traditions describe tantra as the most devoted and intense of all the traditions of Hinduism; it is even more so than the extremely rigorous requirements demanded of the priesthood among the many temples.

Eastern people view Witches as providers of services just as necessary as a plumber or doctor.

Tantrics are expected to devote their entire lives to the pursuit of enlightenment. Tales abound in Hindu folklore about tantrics who became distracted on their way to enlightenment and went mad with the power. The prevalence of these tales causes the folk to both fear and revere tantric Witches. The unusual lifestyle of these Witches breeds both admiration and suspicion. People see Witches as holding the power to resolve their problems. Rumors abound about the powers of tantrics; levitation, the power to cast curses in fits of anger, and near immortality all color the practices of these individuals. None outside tantric study know whether these people truly have power, or simply possess skill with smoke and mirrors. The tantrics and Witches themselves never answer these questions.

Indian Witches generally live in villages apart from their neighbors—remote, but still locatable. Some Witches, however, live in the cremation yards year round—taboo to all others in

Indian society. It is thought that the people who choose to live at these sites gather power through their exposure to the ashes of the dead, though again there is little evidence to support such ideas.

Witches do not enjoy universal acceptance throughout India. In poverty-laden areas, stoning is common for someone accused of practicing of Witchcraft. In other areas, a Witch is usually feared enough that townspeople will leave him or her alone. Sometimes, however, the accusation of a witchcraft actually is a manifestation of hatred or greed. That is, unscrupulous families may, for instance, accuse a daughter-in-law of the practice so the town can kill her and they will not have another mouth to feed.

Mansi Suresh, a Hindu born in India whom I interviewed for this article, explains the distinctions and treatment regarding Witches in India thusly: "It is much like Voudon in the United States. People only look at the magical practices and assume that it's something frightening. These people never admit it, but they do go to these Witches that they're so afraid of for help in getting curses lifted, practicing exorcisms and correcting bad luck."

At times, Suresh says, Witches are revered in India as an important stabilizing force; other times they are feared. Witches in India clean up the psychic sludge of the society. Their ability to do so both frightens and fascinates those who call upon them for services. Suresh believes her family once experienced an attack from a Witch.

"We would find little black drawings in our house, and pieces of cloth that had fruits and nuts wrapped in them," she said. The reason for the cursing, as far as she could tell, turned out to be a mentally unbalanced woman's desire for her family's property. Priyanka, Mansi's sister, believes that this Witch continues her malice. "I always know when she's been working—I have nightmares, and my life always hits its lowest points at those times."

Despite the worry about curses and other attacks, practices normally associated with Witchcraft in Western culture also receive complete cultural legitimacy in India. For instance, priests must learn to read Vedic astrological charts in order to assist families in making decisions regarding arranged marriages and other important rites. Astrology is viewed universally as a legitimate career, and Hindu families rely on astrologers heavily for major life decisions. Often a family visits an astrologer before visiting a priest, and priests take the charts made by astrologers and identify the long-term karmic issues that a family may experience.

"My mother's brother was having all sorts of problems," continues Mansi Suresh. "The men in his family kept dying, and when he went to a priest he discovered that a curse had been laid upon all the men in his family."

Suresh's uncle set about resolving his problem by visiting a Witch who determined that the curse came from some action of one of his ancestors. She lifted the curse, and the man and his sons continue to live in good health in India.

Witchcraft in India is not a role a person can choose. It is strictly a hereditary path, and a difficult path—one that often leads to social isolation. The people who practice this art are very necessary to the social fabric of the Indian nation, but they also sometimes suffer for their traditions. The associations with death and destruction gods trigger fear, as does the awareness that some of these Witches, the women in particular, have great power.

Still, in a country where the status of a human being can vary province by province, the existence and role of Witches can also vary in safety and status. In one part of the country, such knowledge can endanger life; in another part, it can ensure safety and support.

Corn: The Spirit of Summer

by Elizabeth Barrette

The corn is tasseling outside as I write this. I live in farm country, our house surrounded on all sides by fields of corn and soybeans. Every summer the air fills with pollen. Summer nights are warm and breezy, and the wind carries the pollen a long way. Sometimes in the lazy afternoon, when the breeze is just right, you can see the stuff unrolling like yellow scarves above the cornfields. You sweat, and golden dust clings to your skin.

Corn pollen has a sleepy, sensual smell—like a lover lazily rolling over the rumpled sheets. If you've never smelled it, there's really nothing else like it on Earth.

87

The scent fills the air, sweet and thick, like buttered honey. This is the smell of summer for me, even more evocative than fresh-mown hay or Sun-baked sidewalks or cotton candy at the fair.

In summer, the corn stands tall, taller than a person. The leaves are a deep green, touched with blue, and the silks are brilliant—gold and red slowly turning brown. The tassels atop the stalks look like yellow television antennas, but this is a false impression, as they're dispersing rather than collecting. It's the silks, moist and sticky, each strand connecting to a single kernel, that capture the pollen.

Corn pollen has a sleepy, sensual smell—like a lover lazily rolling over the rumpled sheets.

In the summer, gardens fill with sweet corn. The ears come in early and plump up fast. At farmer's markets and corner lots, pickup trucks sit with their tailgates down, spilling their bounty into waiting hands. Strip back the husks and you can see the kernels shining in the Sun—white like little pearls, yellow like nuggets of gold.

Summer Time Is Corn Time

Summer is a time for eating corn-on-the-cob, roasted fresh from the field and slathered with butter. It is also a time for stocking away creamed corn and niblets for winter. The inherent messiness of corn-on-the cob, and the exuberance of its flavor, perfectly match the gleeful abandon of the season. The Indian corn and the popcorn will come in later, its ripening a sure sign of autumn. But for now, the air still drips with the scent of pollen, a promise of the harvest yet to come.

When the withering heat of the day has faded, I like to slip outside. The fireflies wink and weave in the tall grass. Overhead the stars chip their way through the blue enamel bowl of the sky. And in the deepening twilight, the fields of corn rustle and whisper in the wind. As the corn spirits speak, I listen.

Types of Corn

Corn comes in many varieties, developed over thousands of years. Most of this abundance we owe to Native American farmers. Today we have sweet corn, field corn, Indian corn, and popcorn among other varieties. They each have their own blooming times, their own genes, their own characteristics—but unlike most plants, corn plants are gregarious. Any cultivars that bloom at the same time will cross-pollinate, and this often can wreck the crop.

Sweet corn depends on three main genes to determine its flavor. The "sugary" gene (SU) gives an average amount of sugar that rapidly converts to starch after harvest. The "sugary enhancer" gene (SE) raises the initial amount of sugar, giving a sweeter corn; it also tends to produce more tender kernels. Antique cultivars depend on one of these genes, and so do some modern cultivars. Popular examples include the Silver Queen, Sugar Buns, and Double Standard varieties. The "supersweet" gene (SH) gives a high amount of sugar that does not readily convert to starch, but that does burn up—and as that happens, the kernels get tougher. Supersweet cultivars like Kandy Korn are often inedible later.

Sweet corn comes in white, yellow, and bicolor varieties. Field corn, also called dent corn, comprises one of the primary commercial crops in the United States. People use it both for making food products and industrial products. It is usually yellow, occasionally white. Most of it now comes from seed companies as proprietary hybrids. Indian corn, also called flint corn, has a hard outer shell. It grows well in the Southwest, and in Central and South America. Many varieties are resistant to heat and drought. It comes in yellow, white, red, blue, and multicolor varieties. This is the corn most often sold for harvest decoration.

Popcorn has very low sugar and high starch. Each kernel contains some water inside a very tough shell. When heated, the water turns to steam, causing the kernels to explode into the familiar shape. Popcorn comes mainly in yellow and white, but also a red "strawberry" variety.

Will the Real Corn God Please Stand Up?

Many Native American tribes honor corn in some fashion. This honors, above all else, the centuries of careful breeding by Native farmers who coaxed plump ears out of hardscrabble dirt. Corn formed a staple part of the diet in some tribes. Today you can still get traditional foods like kettle corn (popcorn popped in an iron cauldron) and corn cakes (similar to cornbread) at pow-wows and historical fairs. The "corn spirit" appears in different forms across the Americas.

In the eastern and central regions, the Algonquin tell stories about Onatah, the Corn Maiden, whom an evil spirit abducted and held underground until the Sun found her. The Pawnee hold a peacemaking ceremony called the *Hako,* in which Uti Hiata, Mother Corn, plays a central role. A Shawnee myth involves the discovery that Corn Person is a woman; a man insults her by copulating with the corn, which all disappears from the field. The Cherokee also have a Corn Mother, who cut open her breast so the grain could spring forth and feed her people.

In Iroquois and Seneca mythology, the *Deohako* are spirits of corn, squash, and beans who live together in a single mound. The Cherokee honor Selu, whose name means Corn. They refer to June as *Tihaluhiyi,* or "green corn Moon," and July as *Guyegwoni,* or "ripe corn Moon." The art of Tina Le Marque includes pictures of the Blue Corn Woman, the Blue Corn Maiden, the Green Corn Woman, the Red Corn Woman, and the Yellow Corn Maiden.

In the Southwest, one Navajo myth cites First Man as the spirit of White Corn, First Woman as the spirit of Yellow Corn, and their children as Blue Corn Boy and Many-Colored Corn Girl. In Hopi tradition, the kachina Ahulani always appears in Winter Solstice dances accompanied by his sisters, Yellow Corn Girl and Blue Corn Girl. Among the Tewa Pueblo, the first mothers were White Corn Woman, the mother of winter, and Blue Corn Woman, the mother of summer.

In Central and South America, the Aztecs had a host of deities related to corn. Centeotl was the corn god, also in charge of regeneration. Chicomecoatl was the goddess of corn and fertility. Tlaloc, the god of rain and fertility, lived with the Corn goddesses in a place called Tlalocan. The Mayans had a Corn god represented in many clay figurines. The Peruvians honor the Maize-mother as Zara-mama.

Elsewhere, many deities—including Attis, Osiris, and Demeter—are called "corn gods" or "corn goddesses," but all of these really personify some other grain, as corn comes from the Americas. Only in recent centuries has true corn reached Europe and other parts of the world. So only in America do we find true corn deities: The "real" corn god, or corn goddess, is necessarily a Native American.

Also worth noting is the fact that European references particularly tend to focus on the death of the grain and its spirit, whereas American ones tend to focus on the life and growth of the grain and its spirit. Europe has a myth of "the Dying and Rising God," often spoken of as the Grain God or the Corn God. John Barleycorn is another classic example, and shows the use of "corn" in reference to other grains.

Corn in Religious and Magical Ritual

The same cultures that grow corn and honor its spirit also use various parts of the plant for ceremonies. The Cherokee perform the Green Corn Dance to honor the first harvest of sweet corn. They also use corn for healing, for love spells, in weddings, and in other rituals, and they make poppets from corn shucks. The Navajo use cornmeal and corn pollen as an offering to deities, totems, and the spirits of animals they have hunted, and they use it as a medium in sand paintings. Pollen symbolizes prosperity, peace, and happiness. The Navajo use it to purify and consecrate everything from hogans to people to prayer sticks. The Hopi use corn pollen and kernels in many ceremonies. They also make sacred prayer items called *pahos* from cobs of corn.

In contemporary Pagan culture, corn is used in most of the same applications. Whole ears represent prosperity and fertility; cornmeal and pollen serve a protective role in casting circles.

Many people enjoy making human-shaped cornbreads or cornshuck poppets to represent the Corn God or Corn Goddess. A relatively modern idea is the creation of a Corn Man out of actual corn cobs, suitable for burning in a bonfire during ritual. Corn is ruled by Venus and the element earth, with powers of luck, protection, and divination.

Indeed, many Pagans in America today draw inspiration from the Native American traditions. One Witch I know talks about his experience among the Navajos, and how he made himself a Navajo-style medicine bag using corn pollen and other sacred materials. Others stick to European-style traditions but substitute the local, true corn for European grains such as barley. Corn often appears in Lammas or Mabon rites, and sometimes in Litha rites as well. Pagans also enjoy attending mainstream corn festivals in summer and autumn.

On a sultry summer night, go outside and honor the corn spirits as you know them. Surrender to the power of our native grain. Let yourself sway in time to the whisper of silks and the swish of leaves. Breathe in the hypnotic, enchanting scent of the pollen. Imagine what it would be like to live in a tribe largely dependent on corn for survival, and remember that it remains one of the world's staple crops today.

Corn is a gentle and generous spirit, rarely hostile or stingy unless insulted. Speak to the plants with respect, and they will reward you. Of all the gold that comes from the earth, corn is the most precious.

Land Ho! Pagan Land Sanctuaries of America

by Elizabeth Barrette

In recent decades, Pagans have rarely enjoyed a primary benefit of most other established religions: holy ground. Most of our sacred sites are ancient, made by our ancestors, or they are natural places rather than structures. Most sites also belong to people of other faiths, who are often hostile to us. In the end, we have little access to our own holy places.

But these days, we see a wave of new sacred establishments. Pagan organizations are buying land, raising buildings and stone circles, consecrating shrines—all in the spirit of reclaiming what our ancestors had and creating something for our own descendants. To establish or visit a Pagan land sanctuary is to take your place in a chain of worship reaching into both past and future.

These places offer many benefits. They provide space for us to meet in safety and privacy, without annoying, or being annoyed by, those of differing opinions. They help develop a cohesive culture, pass along cultural material such as music, dance, and ritual techniques to our children and newcomers. They allow us to worship natural spaces, build sacred structures, and protect land from the encroachment of "development." By providing permanence, they make us as Pagans more recognizable to the mainstream as legitimate.

Some sites, particularly those hosting larger festivals, even turn a profit. And the revenues provide church services, improve facilities, and other pleasant perquisites. Most importantly, sacred sites allow us to fulfill our compact with the Earth and with our divine patrons—to cherish and care for the territory and wildlife where we live and worship.

Pilgrimage for Pagans

When you plan to visit a Pagan land sanctuary, first consider your purpose. Do you want to meet other Pagans, or the land itself? Do you want to visit a special shrine, celebrate a holy day, mark a life passage, scatter the ashes of a departed loved one, or form a long-term bond with a particular place and its people? Do you simply want to sit in silence and open yourself to the divine? Your answer will give you a good idea where to start. You can also see below for possible destinations.

The next step is to cultivate a spirit of reverence. In pilgrimage, travel often proves as meaningful as arrival. Watch and listen along the way for messages from your patron deities, totems, ancestors, or other guiding spirits. Remember the words of White Buffalo Calf Woman: "In a sacred manner I walk."

Do you walk in a sacred manner? If not, what would you change? Meditate on this before before, during, and after the trip.

The difference between a tourist and a pilgrim is that a tourist mainly takes and a pilgrim mainly gives. A tourist takes a vacation, pictures, souvenirs. A pilgrim gives attention, donations of money or services, tokens of bad habits to relinquish and

The difference between a tourist and a pilgrim is that a tourist mainly takes, and a pilgrim gives.

of changes to make. Many ancient holy places are festooned with prayer flags, letters of reverence, coins in sacred springs. Some Pagan sanctuaries have a "blessing tree," wishing well, or other repository for offerings. When packing, take some things to give away—postcards for friends you meet, a stone from your yard to leave at a shrine, a jar of water for a water-sharing ritual, whatever inspiration suggests.

Finally, sustain a sense of gratitude as you travel. Count your blessings. Give thanks for what you have, and for what you do not have—the emptiness still waiting to be filled with new blessings. Express your appreciation to those who help you along the way. Let the spirits of the land know that you come as a pilgrim, not a beggar. That said, here is a list of some Pagan land sanctuaries you might choose to visit.

Sacred Sites to Visit

Brushwood

Brushwood consists of 180 acres, largely forested, located in rural New York a few minutes from the town of Sherman. The campground is clothing-optional and secluded.

Brushwood hosts sabbat festivals for Beltane, Summer Solstice, and Samhain. They have also held Women's Weekends and specialty events like the national meeting of Ar nDraoicht Fein. Brushwood is best known for the Starwood festival, celebrating its twenty-fifth year in 2005. Weekends not occupied by other events are available for general camping.

Amenities include two pavilions, hot and cold running water with flush toilets and showers, a swimming pool, and a hot

tub. A heated lodge offers additional year-round function space, and sleeping space for around twelve people. There are many activities to enjoy, such as workshops, lectures, performances, rituals, and ceremonies. This site does not permit pets.

Brushwood events do not offer childcare or babysitting services. However, there is a play area where parents can take their children, as long as parents provide their own supervision. For more information visit: http://www.brushwood.com.

Circle Sanctuary Nature Preserve

The Circle Sanctuary Nature Preserve consists of 200 acres, mostly wooded and hilly in southwestern Wisconsin near Mount Horeb (in an area known as the "driftless bioregion"). Selena Fox founded Circle Sanctuary in 1974, and the preserve in 1983. It achieved sacred land zoning in 1988.

The scenic preserve is a patchwork of prairies, forests, springs and wetlands, rock outcroppings, and developed spaces for human use. West Blue Mounds Creek runs across the land. Circle Sanctuary and its natural grounds serve a variety of purposes—including research, spiritual healing and education, support of existing ecosystems, and a place for humans to deepen their connections to nature.

Although not open for drop-in visits, this site hosts a number of workshops, meditations, and other events. These include the annual Earth Day Celebration, the sabbats, several different study circles that meet monthly, and so forth. Work Days are held on Saturdays. For more information visit: http://www.circlesanctuary.org.

Dragon Hills

Dragon Hills consists of one-hundred seventy wooded acres in west Georgia near the town of Bowden. The central forty acres are clothing-optional; the outer area clothing-required.

This site offers unlimited shaded camping space. On the boundaries of the site are electrical hookups for recreational vehicles and limited electrical outlets, available by advance arrangement. Other amenities include the Great Hall (currently under construction), a complete outdoor kitchen, outhouses, heated showers, lake, and spring-fed swimming hole.

Scheduled events include the annual RowanFest, as well as sabbats such as Litha and Samhain. Activities include drumming, dancing, bonfires, workshops, and a bardic circle. You can buy meal tickets at festivals sponsored by Dragon Hills; other events may or may not have meal tickets. Aside from scheduled events, you can rent the site for activities. Dragon Hills is available for handfastings, rituals, private gatherings, weekend retreats, picnics, and so on by arrangement with the management. You can also join work parties before or after a gathering.

Dragon Hills is a family-friendly site. The childcare area includes a kiddie pool, swingsets, and a fenced-in tipi. Childcare and kiddie programming are available during some events. Teens may camp in the separate Teen Campsite with a signed consent form from their parents. Elders may enjoy camping in a reserved area convenient to the privy and showers, and set-up assistance is available by prior arrangement. See: http://dragonhills.com.

Four Quarters

Four Quarters is an InterFaith Church of EarthReligion that lies in the Allegheny mountains of central Pennsylvania. This complex community includes many discrete entities—the church, the farm, the land, the camp—each with its own unique responsibilities and assets.

The main camp is snuggled against a cliff and is lined by Sidling Creek. Near the creek stands the sweat lodge site, which has separate lodges for eclectic and traditional sweats and is shielded from the access road by lush evergreens. Hemlock Hole offers a fine location for natural swimming and for many ceremonies. The drum and fire circle lies at the center of the camp, near the Merchants Village and the camp kitchen. This site can feed 500 people at once; the skilled staff uses top-notch ingredients like local beef and special-order vegetables.

Built into the hillside facing High Meadow, the fully equipped main stage boasts separate vehicle access and a 165-amp 3-phase generator. When powered down, this location also hosts workshops, classes, music, and dancing. Various sites offer camping—some for members, others for visitors—with electric service in certain areas. There are open-air showers, and porta-potties can be brought in for large events.

Most famous, though, is the stone circle. This community is slowly building a megalithic structure every bit as impressive as the ones left to us by our ancestors. The principle is we really shouldn't rest on their laurels, but should make our own contribution to future generations. Many ceremonies take place here.

Four Quarters facilities are available to church and farm members, and to guests for handfastings, family circles, rites of passage, and weekend camping. You can rent anything from a small part of the camp to the whole shebang—including staff to cook the meals. The site also hosts a number of religious gatherings open to the public. Membership in the church is not required in order to use the sanctuary. They have hosted sabbat festival events, as well as for diverse traditions like the African diaspora, trancedancing, sweat lodge intensives, a Spiral Scouts family weekend, and more. Four Quarters also offers Full and New Moon ceremonies.

This InterFaith Church often uses a Wiccan format for rituals but also draws from other EarthReligion sources. Members explore the divine within themselves—in both feminine and masculine aspects. The Church prides itself on offering "safe and sane sacred space" for all. There is no trash service at this site—you must pack out everything that you bring in. There is no clothing policy per se; it varies per event. For more info, visit: http://www.4qf.org.

Mother Rest Sacred Grove
Mother Rest Sacred Grove consists of ten acres of farmland and wetland mixed with nascent forest. It lies in Washington state, about two hours north of Seattle, and has Nest status in the Church of All Worlds.

In 1998, Mother Rest Sacred Grove qualified as the very first Pagan Church Eco-Cemetery in North America, earning recognition from Whatcom County. This sacred nature preserve enjoys protection from future development or abuse so that its Memorial Trees may flourish unmolested. These grow inside a ten-foot-square plot. The plots are suitable for burying or scattering cremated remains. Because the cemetery belongs to a wetland area, no bodies can be interred there.

Two out of the ten acres make up the cemetery proper. The other eight acres offer habitat for wildlife and space for shrines. A creek runs through the land, and the wetland also includes a small pond. These offer lovely locations for ceremony or meditation. Unlike most mainstream cemeteries, Mother Rest Sacred Grove understands the desire of some Pagans to visit during the sabbats, especially Samhain. The land also has two small houses and a barn. For more info, visit: http://www.mrsgrove.com.

Ozark Avalon Church of Nature

The Ozark Avalon Church of Nature lies in central Missouri on the bluffs near the Missouri River. This nature preserve consists of 100 acres of upland forest, open meadow, and wetland.

The attractions of this location include groves, grottoes and natural shrines, hiking trails, and a three-acre lake with space for swimming. Facilities include a sweat lodge, several campgrounds, meadow space for rituals, hot showers, flush toilets and composting toilets, fire rings, picnic tables, and a swimming pool. Limited indoor sleeping space with air conditioning is available. The retreat center also offers a kitchen and dining room, washer and dryer, woodstove, modest library of Pagan books, and Internet access.

Because the congregation consists of many children of all ages, Ozark Avalon is a very family-friendly site. Most events offer at least some childcare and kiddie programming. The retreat center house includes a large fenced area for children to play. Also, elders past the age of sixty-two get a 10 percent discount on all rates. For those interested in more mature topics, some events are restricted to adults only.

Ozark Avalon is a church of Shamanic Wicca. They offer a safe place for indoor and outdoor worship, available to anyone practicing an Earth-centered path. Scheduled events include sabbat festivals, god weekend (men only), goddess weekend (women only), and Interdependence Day. The site has also provided space for particular group events. Work weekends give you a chance to earn credit for festivals.

Those interested in visiting can make their own arrangements. You can reserve the land for private ceremonies such as dedications, handfastings, croning/saging, or coven retreats. On a smaller scale, you can rent a bed-and-breakfast room in the retreat center. General camping is available most of the time, but may be restricted during events. For more information, visit: http://www.ozarkavalon.org.

The Temple of Goddess Spirituality Dedicated to Sekhmet

The Temple of Goddess Spirituality Dedicated to Sekhmet, also known as the Temple of Sekhmet, consists of a small open Temple and a Guest House, with surrounding grounds. The twenty acres of land on which the Temple stands were donated back to the Western Shoshone, who traditionally occupied this territory. It lies in Nevada, about 45 miles northwest of Las Vegas.

The Temple, made of sand-colored stucco, stands open to the elements. Its four arched entrances face the four directions. At sunset and sunrise, long beams of light stretch through the arches. Breezes blow in one, out another. At night, the Moon looks down through the open dome of the roof, made of interlocking copper rings. In the center of the Temple stands a sacred firepit.

The site also includes a fully equipped guest house. In addition to a small number of beds, it has generous floorspace for sleeping. Guests should bring sleeping bags. Tent camping is available near the guest house and elsewhere.

A variety of different groups make use of this site, including followers of the Temple of Goddess Spirituality and the Desert Moon Circle. The Temple hosts a full calendar including all eight sabbats, plus thirteen each New Moons (women only) and Full Moons (mixed genders). Additional events  include Sekhmet Day, Mother's Day, and free Wiccan learning circles. The site is also available for rituals on healing or world peace, and rites of passage. A potluck supper usually follows each ritual.

Please remember and respect the fragility of the desert environment. Walk lightly on the land; pack out what you take in. Leave your pets at home. This is a drug-free, alcohol-free spiritual sanctuary. (http://www.sekhmettemple.com/ or The Temple of Goddess Spirituality, Patricia Pearlman, P.O. Box 946, Indian Springs, NV 89018).

Wisteria

Wisteria consists of 620 acres in southeastern Ohio. It lies in the Allegheny mountain plateau, part of the Appalachian chain. The nature retreat contains over 200 acres. It includes a mix of field and forest, scenic rock outcroppings, streams, caves, abundant wildlife, and trails. Wisteria also incorporates some reclaimed land, helping it recover from previous surface-mining. A residential area encompasses the homes of Wisteria families, who work towards cooperative stewardship of common ground. Site facilities include a stage, pavilion, workshop space, swimming pond, and the Turtle Mound.

The campground stays open from May 1 through October 31. Wisteria hosts a variety of events—including concerts, festivals, retreats, workshops, work weekends, and general weekend camping. Best known are the Wisteria Music Festival and the Pagan Spirit Festival, which are run by Circle Sanctuary (see above) but held on Wisteria's larger site. The event campground is available for gatherings large and small—such as handfastings or music festivals.

Wisteria rents space to organizations who demonstrate environmental consciousness and respect for nature. You can rent the whole campground for private camping events, with site maintenance and services provided by Wisteria staff. For more information visit: http://wisteria.org.

In Conclusion

Pagan land sanctuaries restore to us the sense of permanence, continuity, and connection with the Earth that our ancestors enjoyed. Today, you can find a sacred site for almost every need in most parts of the United States. Others are springing up in other countries as well. By your presence, your donations of money or labor, your word-of-mouth recommendations to friends, and your spiritual energy, you help to support our growing network of holy ground.

There are as many reasons and ways of making pilgrimage as there are pilgrims. But I think T. S. Eliot said it best:

> *We shall not cease from exploration*
> *And the end of all our exploring*
> *Will be to arrive where we started*
> *And know the place for the first time.*

Almanac Section

spring 2004 – spring 2005

The days & the nights, the Moon & the stars, the colors & the energies, & all the latest Wiccan/Pagan news; the yearly almanac gives you everything you need to get you through this heady astrological year

With news items written by S. Tifulcrum

spring 2004 – spring 2005

spring 2004 – spring 2005

spring 2005

What's Listed in the Almanac
(and How to Use It)

In these listings you will find the date, lunar phase, Moon sign, color, and magical influence for the day.

The Day

Each day is ruled by a planet that possesses specific magical influences:

Monday (Moon): Peace, sleep, healing, compassion, friends, psychic awareness, purification, and fertility.

Tuesday (Mars): Passion, sex, courage, aggression, and protection.

Wednesday (Mercury): The conscious mind, study, travel, divination, and wisdom.

Thursday (Jupiter): Expansion, money, prosperity, and generosity.

Friday (Venus): Love, friendship, reconciliation, and beauty.

Saturday (Saturn): Longevity, exorcism, endings, homes, and houses.

Sunday (Sun): Healing, spirituality, success, strength, and protection.

The Lunar Phase

The lunar phase is important in determining the best times for magic.

The Waxing Moon (from the New Moon to the Full) is the ideal time for magic to draw things toward you.

The Full Moon is the time of greatest power.

The Waning Moon (from the Full Moon to the New) is a time for study, meditation, and little magical work (except magic designed to banish harmful energies).

The Moon's Sign

The Moon continuously "moves" through the zodiac, from Aries to Pisces. Each sign possesses its own significance:

Aries: Good for initiating things, but lacks staying power and quickly passes. People tend to be argumentative and assertive.

Taurus: Things begun now are lasting, tend to increase in value, and are hard to alter. Appreciation for beauty and sensory experience.

Gemini: Things begun now are easily changed by outside influence. Time for shortcuts, communication, games, and fun.

Cancer: Stimulates emotional rapport between people. Pinpoints need, supports growth and nurturance. Tends to domestic concerns.

Leo: Draws emphasis to the self, to central ideas or institutions, away from connections with others and emotional needs. People tend to be melodramatic.

Virgo: Favors accomplishment of details and commands from higher up. Focuses on health, hygiene, and daily schedules.

Libra: Favors cooperation, social activities, beautification of surroundings, balance, and partnership.

Scorpio: Increases awareness of psychic power. Precipitates psychic crises and ends connections thoroughly. People tend to brood and become secretive.

Sagittarius: Encourages flights of imagination and confidence. This is an adventurous, philosophical, and athletic Moon sign. Favors expansion and growth.

Capricorn: Develops strong structure. Focus on traditions, responsibilities, and obligations. A good time to set boundaries and rules.

Aquarius: Rebellious energy. Time to break habits and make abrupt change. Personal freedom and individuality is the focus.

Pisces: The focus is on dreaming, nostalgia, intuition, and psychic impressions. A good time for spiritual or philanthropic activities.

Color and Incense

The colors for the day are based on information from *Personal Alchemy* by Amber Wolfe, and relate to the planet that rules each day. This information can be taken into consideration along with other factors when blending magic into mundane life.

Time Changes

The times and dates of astrological phenomena in this almanac are based on Eastern Standard Time (EST) and Eastern Daylight Saving Time (EDT). If you live outside the Eastern Time Zone, or in a place that does not use Daylight Saving Time, adjust your times:

Pacific Standard Time: Subtract three hours.

Mountain Standard Time: Subtract two hours.

Central Standard Time: Subtract one hour.

Alaska/Hawaii: Subtract five hours.

Areas that have no Daylight Saving Time: Subtract an extra hour from the time given. Daylight Saving Time runs from April 4, 2004 to October 31, 2004.

Key to Astrological Signs

Planets		Signs	
☉	Sun	♈	Aries
♃	Jupiter	♉	Taurus
☽	Moon	♊	Gemini
♄	Saturn	♋	Cancer
☿	Mercury	♌	Leo
♅	Uranus	♍	Virgo
♀	Venus	♎	Libra
♆	Neptune	♏	Scorpio
♂	Mars	♐	Sagittarius
♇	Pluto	♑	Capricorn
		♒	Aquarius
		♓	Pisces

Festivals and Holidays

Festivals are listed throughout the year. The exact dates of many of these ancient festivals are difficult to determine; prevailing data has been used.

2004–2005 Sabbats and Full Moons

March 20, 2004	Ostara (Spring Equinox)
April 5	Full Moon 7:03 am
May 1	Beltane
May 4	Full Moon 4:33 pm
June 3	Full Moon 12:20 am
June 20	Litha (Summer Solstice)
July 2	Full Moon 7:09 am
July 31	Full Moon 2:05 pm
August 1	Lammas
August 29	Full Moon 10:22 pm
September 22	Mabon (Fall Equinox)
September 28	Full Moon 9:09 am
October 27	Full Moon 11:07 pm
October 31	Samhain
November 26	Full Moon 3:07 pm
December 21	Yule (Winter Solstice)
December 26	Full Moon 10:06 am
January 25, 2005	Full Moon 5:32 am
February 2	Imbolc
February 23	Full Moon 11:54 pm
March 20	Ostara (Spring Equinox)

March 2004
Spring Equinox · March 20

Saturday

March 20 ♄

Ostara · Spring Equinox · Int'l Astrology Day

Waning Moon

Color: Indigo

Moon Sign: Pisces

Moon Phase: New Moon 5:41 pm

Sun enters Aries 1:49 am

Moon enters Aries 4:29 pm

Sunday

March 21

Juarez Day (Mexican)

Waxing Moon

Color: Gold

Moon Sign: Aries

Moon Phase: First Quarter

☽   **March 22**

Hilaria (Roman)   Moon Sign: Aries
Waxing Moon   Moon Phase: First Quarter
Color: Ivory

♂   **March 23**

Pakistan Day   Moon Sign: Aries
Waxing Moon   Moon Phase: First Quarter
Color: White   Moon enters Taurus 1:10 am

☿   **March 24**

Day of Blood (Roman)   Moon Sign: Taurus
Waxing Moon   Moon Phase: First Quarter
Color: Yellow

♃   **March 25**

Tichborne Dole (English)   Moon Sign: Taurus
Waxing Moon   Moon Phase: First Quarter
Color: Turquoise   Moon enters Gemini 12:35 pm

♀   **March 26**

Prince Kuhio Day (Hawaiian)   Moon Sign: Gemini
Waxing Moon   Moon Phase: First Quarter
Color: Purple

♄   **March 27**

Smell the Breezes Day (Egyptian)   Moon Sign: Gemini
Waxing Moon   Moon Phase: First Quarter
Color: Blue

☉   **March 28**

Oranges and Lemons Service (English)   Moon Sign: Gemini
Waxing Moon   Moon Phase: Second Quarter 6:48 pm
Color: Orange   Moon enters Cancer 1:23 am

March 29 ☽

St. Eustace's Day
Waxing Moon
Color: Gray

Moon Sign: Cancer
Moon Phase: Second Quarter

March 30 ♂

Seward's Day (Alaskan)
Waxing Moon
Color: Scarlet

Moon Sign: Cancer
Moon Phase: Second Quarter
Moon enters Leo 1:07 pm

March 31 ☿

The Borrowed Days (European)
Waxing Moon
Color: Brown

Moon Sign: Leo
Moon Phase: Second Quarter

News Item

Colorado School District Asks: "Is yoga religion or exercise?"

The Aspen, Colorado, school district announced recent plans to teach yoga as part of its educational curriculum, but a local Christian pastor claimed yoga was religious and therefore should not be taught in school. Despite the citation of four court rulings that indicated yoga violated separation of church and state, the Aspen school district board had voted 3 to 1 in favor of the yoga curriculum. Their decision was reinforced by favorable responses toward yoga education by other clergy, who said it would be taught as exercise, not religion. Implementation of the program will wait until the curriculum has been reviewed and approved by the school district's attorney.

April 2004

♃   April 1

April Fools' Day   Moon Sign: Leo
Waxing Moon   Moon Phase: Second Quarter
Color: Green   Moon enters Virgo 9:45 pm

Thursday

♀   April 2

The Battle of Flowers (French)   Moon Sign: Virgo
Waxing Moon   Moon Phase: Second Quarter
Color: Pink

Friday

♄   April 3

Thirteenth Day Out (Iranian)   Moon Sign: Virgo
Waxing Moon   Moon Phase: Second Quarter
Color: Indigo

Saturday

☉   April 4

Daylight Saving Time begins · Palm Sunday   Moon Sign: Virgo
Waxing Moon   Moon Phase: Second Quarter
Color: Yellow   Moon enters Libra 3:52 am

Sunday

Monday
Tuesday
Wednesday
Thursday
Friday
Saturday
Sunday

April 5 ☽

Tomb-Sweeping Day (Chinese) Moon Sign: Libra
Waxing Moon Moon Phase: Full Moon 7:03 am
Color: Lavender

April 6 ♂

Passover begins Moon Sign: Libra
Waning Moon Moon Phase: Third Quarter
Color: White Moon enters Scorpio 4:36 am

April 7 ☿

Festival of Pure Brightness (Chinese) Moon Sign: Scorpio
Waning Moon Moon Phase: Third Quarter
Color: Topaz

April 8 ♃

Buddha's Birthday Moon Sign: Scorpio
Waning Moon Moon Phase: Third Quarter
Color: Crimson Moon enters Sagittarius 7:50 am

April 9 ♀

Good Friday · Orthodox Good Friday Moon Sign: Sagittarius
Waning Moon Moon Phase: Third Quarter
Color: Purple

April 10 ♄

The Tenth of April (English) Moon Sign: Sagittarius
Waning Moon Moon Phase: Third Quarter
Color: Black Moon enters Capricorn 9:33 am

April 11 ☉

Easter · Orthodox Easter Moon Sign: Capricorn
Waning Moon Moon Phase: Fourth Quarter 11:46 pm
Color: Gold

☽ April 12

Passover ends · Cerealia (Roman)
Waning Moon
Color: Silver

Moon Sign: Capricorn
Moon Phase: Fourth Quarter
Moon enters Aquarius 12:33 pm

♂ April 13

Thai New Year
Waning Moon
Color: Red

Moon Sign: Aquarius
Moon Phase: Fourth Quarter

☿ April 14

Sanno Festival (Japanese)
Waning Moon
Color: White

Moon Sign: Aquarius
Moon Phase: Fourth Quarter
Moon enters Pisces 5:24 pm

♃ April 15

Plowing Festival (Chinese)
Waning Moon
Color: Purple

Moon Sign: Pisces
Moon Phase: Fourth Quarter

♀ April 16

Zurich Spring Festival (Swiss)
Waning Moon
Color: Coral

Moon Sign: Pisces
Moon Phase: Fourth Quarter

♄ April 17

Yayoi Matsuri (Japanese)
Waning Moon
Color: Gray

Moon Sign: Pisces
Moon Phase: Fourth Quarter
Moon enters Aries 12:24 am

☉ April 18

Flower Festival (Japanese)
Waning Moon
Color: Orange

Moon Sign: Aries
Moon Phase: Fourth Quarter

April 19 ☽

Women's Celebration (Balinese)
Waning Moon
Color: Ivory

Moon Sign: Aries
Moon Phase: New Moon 9:21 am
Moon enters Taurus 9:43 am
Sun enters Taurus 1:50 pm

April 20 ♂

Drum Festival (Japanese)
Waxing Moon
Color: Black

Moon Sign: Taurus
Moon Phase: First Quarter

April 21 ☿

Tiradentes Day (Brazilian)
Waxing Moon
Color: Brown

Moon Sign: Taurus
Moon Phase: First Quarter
Moon enters Gemini 9:10 pm

April 22 ♃

Earth Day
Waxing Moon
Color: Turquoise

Moon Sign: Gemini
Moon Phase: First Quarter

April 23 ♀

St. George's Day (English)
Waxing Moon
Color: White

Moon Sign: Gemini
Moon Phase: First Quarter

April 24 ♄

St. Mark's Eve
Waxing Moon
Color: Blue

Moon Sign: Gemini
Moon Phase: First Quarter
Moon enters Cancer 9:56 am

April 25 ☉

Robigalia (Roman)
Waxing Moon
Color: Amber

Moon Sign: Cancer
Moon Phase: First Quarter

☽   April 26

Arbor Day   Moon Sign: Cancer
Waxing Moon   Moon Phase: First Quarter
Color: Gray   Moon enters Leo 10:14 pm

♂   April 27

Humabon's Conversion (Filipino)   Moon Sign: Leo
Waxing Moon   Moon Phase: Second Quarter 1:32 pm
Color: Scarlet

☿   April 28

Floralia (Roman)   Moon Sign: Leo
Waxing Moon   Moon Phase: Second Quarter
Color: Yellow

♃   April 29

Green Day (Japanese)   Moon Sign: Leo
Waxing Moon   Moon Phase: Second Quarter
Color: White   Moon enters Virgo 8:00 am

♀   April 30

Walpurgis Night · May Eve   Moon Sign: Virgo
Waxing Moon   Moon Phase: Second Quarter
Color: Rose

May 2004

News Item

Chinese Use Spirituality to Fight SARS

In May 2003, Chinese health officials reported that at least 262 people on China's mainland had been killed from Severe Acute Respiratory Syndrome, or SARS, and another 5,000 were infected by the disease. With the government seemingly unable to do much to halt the spread of SARS, Chinese people across the country turned increasingly to alternative forms of healing and protection—particularly those in the supernatural and spiritual realms. Methods of seeking protection included lighting firecrackers, visiting sorcerers, bowing to scrolls or statues, and striking gongs or drums. Most of the people employing these techniques were farmers who knew little of the science behind SARS and relied instead on local folk wisdom.

May 1   ♄

Beltane · May Day	Moon Sign: Virgo
Waxing Moon	Moon Phase: Second Quarter
Color: Indigo	Moon enters Libra 2:03 pm

May 2

Big Kite Flying (Japanese)	Moon Sign: Libra
Waxing Moon	Moon Phase: Second Quarter
Color: Orange	

☽ May 3

Holy Cross Day
Waxing Moon
Color: Lavender

Moon Sign: Libra
Moon Phase: Second Quarter
Moon enters Scorpio 4:38 pm

♂ May 4

Bona Dea (Roman)
Waxing Moon
Color: Black

Moon Sign: Scorpio
Moon Phase: Full Moon 4:33 pm

☿ May 5

Cinco de Mayo (Mexican)
Waning Moon
Color: Brown

Moon Sign: Scorpio
Moon Phase: Third Quarter
Moon enters Sagittarius 5:08 pm

♃ May 6

Martyrs' Day (Lebanese)
Waning Moon
Color: Green

Moon Sign: Sagittarius
Moon Phase: Third Quarter

♀ May 7

Pilgrimage of St. Nicholas (Italian)
Waning Moon
Color: Pink

Moon Sign: Sagittarius
Moon Phase: Third Quarter
Moon enters Capricorn 5:17 pm

♄ May 8

Liberation Day (French)
Waning Moon
Color: Gray

Moon Sign: Capricorn
Moon Phase: Third Quarter

☉ May 9

Mother's Day
Waning Moon
Color: Gold

Moon Sign: Capricorn
Moon Phase: Third Quarter
Moon enters Aquarius 6:46 pm

May 10 ☽

First Day of Bird Week (Japanese)
Waning Moon
Color: White

Moon Sign: Aquarius
Moon Phase: Third Quarter

May 11 ♂

Ukai Season Opens (Japanese)
Waning Moon
Color: Red

Moon Sign: Aquarius
Moon Phase: Fourth Quarter 7:04 am
Moon enters Pisces 10:52 pm

May 12 ☿

Florence Nightingale's Birthday
Waning Moon
Color: Yellow

Moon Sign: Pisces
Moon Phase: Fourth Quarter

May 13 ♃

Pilgrimage to Fatima (Portuguese)
Waning Moon
Color: Turquoise

Moon Sign: Pisces
Moon Phase: Fourth Quarter

May 14 ♀

Carabao Festival (Spanish)
Waning Moon
Color: Purple

Moon Sign: Pisces
Moon Phase: Fourth Quarter
Moon enters Aries 6:02 am

May 15 ♄

Festival of St. Dympna (Belgian)
Waning Moon
Color: Blue

Moon Sign: Aries
Moon Phase: Fourth Quarter

May 16 ☉

St. Honoratus' Day
Waning Moon
Color: Amber

Moon Sign: Aries
Moon Phase: Fourth Quarter
Moon enters Taurus 3:57 pm

☽

May 17

Norwegian Independence Day
Waning Moon
Color: Silver

Moon Sign: Taurus
Moon Phase: Fourth Quarter

♂

May 18

Las Piedras Day (Uruguayan)
Waning Moon
Color: Gray

Moon Sign: Taurus
Moon Phase: Fourth Quarter

☿

May 19

Pilgrimage to Treguier (French)
Waning Moon
Color: White

Moon Sign: Taurus
Moon Phase: New Moon 12:52 am
Moon enters Gemini 3:47 am

♃

May 20

Pardon of the Singers (British)
Waxing Moon
Color: Purple

Moon Sign: Gemini
Moon Phase: First Quarter
Sun enters Gemini 12:59 pm

♀

May 21

Victoria Day (Canadian)
Waxing Moon
Color: Rose

Moon Sign: Gemini
Moon Phase: First Quarter
Moon enters Cancer 4:35 pm

♄

May 22

Heroes' Day (Sri Lankan)
Waxing Moon
Color: Black

Moon Sign: Cancer
Moon Phase: First Quarter

☉

May 23

Tubilustrium (Roman)
Waxing Moon
Color: Yellow

Moon Sign: Cancer
Moon Phase: First Quarter

May 24

Culture Day (Bulgarian)
Waxing Moon
Color: Ivory

☽

Moon Sign: Cancer
Moon Phase: First Quarter
Moon enters Leo 5:07 am

May 25

Lady Godiva's Day
Waxing Moon
Color: White

♂

Moon Sign: Leo
Moon Phase: First Quarter

May 26

Shavuot
Waxing Moon
Color: Topaz

☿

Moon Sign: Leo
Moon Phase: First Quarter
Moon enters Virgo 3:52 pm

May 27

Saint Augustine of Canterbury's Day
Waxing Moon
Color: Crimson

♃

Moon Sign: Virgo
Moon Phase: Second Quarter 3:57 am

May 28

St. Germain's Day
Waxing Moon
Color: Coral

♀

Moon Sign: Virgo
Moon Phase: Second Quarter
Moon enters Libra 11:22 pm

May 29

Royal Oak Day (English)
Waxing Moon
Color: Indigo

♄

Moon Sign: Libra
Moon Phase: Second Quarter

May 30

Pentecost
Waxing Moon
Color: Gold

☉

Moon Sign: Libra
Moon Phase: Second Quarter

⊙   **May 31**

Memorial Day (observed)   Moon Sign: Libra
Waxing Moon   Moon Phase: Second Quarter
Color: Gray   Moon enters Scorpio 3:08 am

Monday

News Item

Pagan Student Refuses to Take Part in School-Sanctioned Religious Activities

India Tracy, a fourteen-year-old straight-A student from Union, Tennessee, has repeatedly been punished for refusing to participate in school-sanctioned religious activities. Tracy and her family are Pagan, and have filed a $300,000 lawsuit asking for damages to pay India's tuition to a private school, legal fees, and the cost of psychological counseling. The suit also seeks a court prohibition against "the school system's continued religious indoctrination of children." Among other things, Tracy refused to participate in the Area Wide Crusade sponsored by a local Baptist congregation and held during school hours. Tracy is currently being homeschooled.

June 2004

Tuesday

June 1 ♂

National Day (Tunisian) Moon Sign: Scorpio
Waxing Moon Moon Phase: Second Quarter
Color: Black

Wednesday

June 2 ☿

Rice Harvest Festival (Malaysian) Moon Sign: Scorpio
Waxing Moon Moon Phase: Second Quarter
Color: Yellow Moon enters Sagittarius 3:52 am

Thursday

June 3 ♃

Memorial to Broken Dolls (Japanese) Moon Sign: Sagittarius
Waxing Moon Moon Phase: Full Moon 12:20 am
Color: Green

Friday

June 4 ♀

Full Moon Day (Burmese) Moon Sign: Sagittarius
Waning Moon Moon Phase: Third Quarter
Color: White Moon enters Capricorn 3:12 am

Saturday

June 5 ♄

Constitution Day (Danish) Moon Sign: Capricorn
Waning Moon Moon Phase: Third Quarter
Color: Brown

Sunday

June 6 ☉

Swedish Flag Day Moon Sign: Capricorn
Waning Moon Moon Phase: Third Quarter
Color: Orange Moon enters Aquarius 3:10 am

☽ **June 7**

St. Robert of Newminster's Day
Waning Moon
Color: Lavender

Moon Sign: Aquarius
Moon Phase: Third Quarter

Monday

♂ **June 8**

St. Medard's Day (Belgian)
Waning Moon
Color: Scarlet

Moon Sign: Aquarius
Moon Phase: Third Quarter
Moon enters Pisces 5:38 am

Tuesday

☿ **June 9**

Vestalia (Roman)
Waning Moon
Color: Brown

Moon Sign: Pisces
Moon Phase: Fourth Quarter 4:02 pm

Wednesday

♃ **June 10**

Time-Observance Day (Chinese)
Waning Moon
Color: Turquoise

Moon Sign: Pisces
Moon Phase: Fourth Quarter
Moon enters Aries 11:49 am

Thursday

♀ **June 11**

Kamehameha Day (Hawaiian)
Waning Moon
Color: Pink

Moon Sign: Aries
Moon Phase: Fourth Quarter

Friday

♄ **June 12**

Independence Day (Filipino)
Waning Moon
Color: Blue

Moon Sign: Aries
Moon Phase: Fourth Quarter
Moon enters Taurus 9:37 pm

Saturday

☉ **June 13**

St. Anthony of Padua's Day
Waning Moon
Color: Amber

Moon Sign: Taurus
Moon Phase: Fourth Quarter

Sunday

Monday	**June 14**	☽
	Flag Day	Moon Sign: Taurus
	Waning Moon	Moon Phase: Fourth Quarter
	Color: Silver	

Tuesday	**June 15**	♂
	St. Vitus' Day Fires	Moon Sign: Taurus
	Waning Moon	Moon Phase: Fourth Quarter
	Color: Gray	Moon enters Gemini 9:44 am

Wednesday	**June 16**	☿
	Bloomsday (Irish)	Moon Sign: Gemini
	Waning Moon	Moon Phase: Fourth Quarter
	Color: White	

Thursday	**June 17**	♃
	Bunker Hill Day	Moon Sign: Gemini
	Waning Moon	Moon Phase: New Moon 4:27 pm
	Color: Purple	Moon enters Cancer 10:37 pm

Friday	**June 18**	♀
	Independence Day (Egyptian)	Moon Sign: Cancer
	Waxing Moon	Moon Phase: First Quarter
	Color: Rose	

Saturday	**June 19**	♄
	Juneteenth	Moon Sign: Cancer
	Waxing Moon	Moon Phase: First Quarter
	Color: Black	

Sunday	**June 20**	☉
	Father's Day · Litha · Summer Solstice	Moon Sign: Cancer
	Waxing Moon	Moon Phase: First Quarter
	Color: Gold	Moon enters Leo 11:05 am
		Sun enters Cancer 8:57 pm

☽ June 21
U.S. Constitution Ratified
Waxing Moon
Color: Ivory

Moon Sign: Leo
Moon Phase: First Quarter

♂ June 22
Rose Festival (English)
Waxing Moon
Color: White

Moon Sign: Leo
Moon Phase: First Quarter
Moon enters Virgo 10:10 pm

☿ June 23
St. John's Eve
Waxing Moon
Color: Topaz

Moon Sign: Virgo
Moon Phase: First Quarter

♃ June 24
St. John's Day
Waxing Moon
Color: Crimson

Moon Sign: Virgo
Moon Phase: First Quarter

♀ June 25
Fiesta of Santa Orosia (Spanish)
Waxing Moon
Color: Coral

Moon Sign: Virgo
Moon Phase: Second Quarter 3:08 pm
Moon enters Libra 6:50 am

♄ June 26
Pied Piper Day (German)
Waxing Moon
Color: Indigo

Moon Sign: Libra
Moon Phase: Second Quarter

☉ June 27
Day of the Seven Sleepers (Islamic)
Waxing Moon
Color: Yellow

Moon Sign: Libra
Moon Phase: Second Quarter
Moon enters Scorpio 12:13 pm

June 28 ☽

Paul Bunyan Day
Waxing Moon
Color: Gray

Moon Sign: Scorpio
Moon Phase: Second Quarter

June 29 ♂

Saint Peter and Saint Paul Day
Waxing Moon
Color: Red

Moon Sign: Scorpio
Moon Phase: Second Quarter
Moon enters Sagittarius 2:15 pm

June 30 ☿

The Burning of the Three Firs (French)
Waxing Moon
Color: Brown

Moon Sign: Sagittarius
Moon Phase: Second Quarter

News Item

Bronze Age Remains Found near Stonehenge

In May 2002, archeologists unearthed the remains of a Bronze Age archer who was quickly dubbed the "King of Stonehenge" due to the incredible richness of the burial site. In 2003, researchers subsequently uncovered six more bodies near Stonehenge—four adults and two children. The archer was identified to have come from the Swiss Alps, and the newly discovered remains have been dated as contemporary with those of the archer. The group is thought to have lived around 2300 B.C.—at a time when Britain was moving from the Stone Age into the Bronze Age, and Stonehenge itself was still under construction.

July 2004

♃   July 1

Climbing Mount Fuji (Japanese)
Waxing Moon
Color: White

Moon Sign: Sagittarius
Moon Phase: Second Quarter
Moon enters Capricorn 8:13 am

♀   July 2

Heroes' Day (Zambian)
Waxing Moon
Color: Purple

Moon Sign: Capricorn
Moon Phase: Full Moon 7:09 am

♄   July 3

Indian Sun Dance (Native American)
Waning Moon
Color: Black

Moon Sign: Capricorn
Moon Phase: Third Quarter
Moon enters Aquarius 1:22 pm

☉   July 4

Independence Day
Waning Moon
Color: Orange

Moon Sign: Aquarius
Moon Phase: Third Quarter

July 5 ☽

Monday

Tynwald (Nordic)
Waning Moon
Color: Ivory

Moon Sign: Aquarius
Moon Phase: Third Quarter
Moon enters Pisces 2:26 pm

July 6 ♂

Tuesday

Khao Phansa Day (Thai)
Waning Moon
Color: Scarlet

Moon Sign: Pisces
Moon Phase: Third Quarter

July 7 ☿

Wednesday

Weaver's Festival (Japanese)
Waning Moon
Color: Yellow

Moon Sign: Pisces
Moon Phase: Third Quarter
Moon enters Aries 7:03 pm

July 8 ♃

Thursday

St. Elizabeth's Day (Portuguese)
Waning Moon
Color: Green

Moon Sign: Aries
Moon Phase: Third Quarter

July 9 ♀

Friday

Battle of Sempach Day (Swiss)
Waning Moon
Color: Pink

Moon Sign: Aries
Moon Phase: Fourth Quarter 3:34 am

July 10 ♄

Saturday

Lady Godiva Day (English)
Waning Moon
Color: Indigo

Moon Sign: Aries
Moon Phase: Fourth Quarter
Moon enters Taurus 3:51 am

July 11 ☉

Sunday

Revolution Day (Mongolian)
Waning Moon
Color: Gold

Moon Sign: Taurus
Moon Phase: Fourth Quarter

☽ **July 12**

Lobster Carnival (Nova Scotian)
Waning Moon
Color: Gray

Moon Sign: Taurus
Moon Phase: Fourth Quarter
Moon enters Gemini 3:45 pm

♂ **July 13**

Festival of the Three Cows (Spanish)
Waning Moon
Color: Black

Moon Sign: Gemini
Moon Phase: Fourth Quarter

☿ **July 14**

Bastille Day (French)
Waning Moon
Color: Brown

Moon Sign: Gemini
Moon Phase: Fourth Quarter

♃ **July 15**

St. Swithin's Day
Waning Moon
Color: Purple

Moon Sign: Gemini
Moon Phase: Fourth Quarter
Moon enters Cancer 4:40 am

♀ **July 16**

Our Lady of Carmel
Waning Moon
Color: White

Moon Sign: Cancer
Moon Phase: Fourth Quarter

♄ **July 17**

Rivera Day (Puerto Rican)
Waning Moon
Color: Blue

Moon Sign: Cancer
Moon Phase: New Moon 7:24 am
Moon enters Leo 4:56 pm

☉ **July 18**

Gion Matsuri Festival (Japanese)
Waxing Moon
Color: Amber

Moon Sign: Leo
Moon Phase: First Quarter

July 19
Monday

Flitch Day (English)
Waxing Moon
Color: Silver

☽

Moon Sign: Leo
Moon Phase: First Quarter

July 20
Tuesday

Binding of Wreaths (Lithuanian)
Waxing Moon
Color: Gray

♂

Moon Sign: Leo
Moon Phase: First Quarter
Moon enters Virgo 3:44 am

July 21
Wednesday

National Day (Belgian)
Waxing Moon
Color: White

☿

Moon Sign: Virgo
Moon Phase: First Quarter

July 22
Thursday

St. Mary Magdalene's Day
Waxing Moon
Color: Crimson

♃

Moon Sign: Virgo
Moon Phase: First Quarter
Sun enters Leo 7:50 am
Moon enters Libra 12:39 pm

July 23
Friday

Mysteries of Santa Cristina (Italian)
Waxing Moon
Color: Coral

♀

Moon Sign: Libra
Moon Phase: First Quarter

July 24
Saturday

Pioneer Day (Mormon)
Waxing Moon
Color: Brown

♄

Moon Sign: Libra
Moon Phase: Second Quarter 7:08 pm
Moon enters Scorpio 7:08 pm

July 25
Sunday

St. James' Day
Waxing Moon
Color: Yellow

☉

Moon Sign: Scorpio
Moon Phase: Second Quarter

☽ **July 26**

St. Anne's Day   Moon Sign: Scorpio
Waxing Moon   Moon Phase: Second Quarter
Color: White   Moon enters Sagittarius 10:48 pm

♂ **July 27**

Sleepyhead Day (Finnish)   Moon Sign: Sagittarius
Waxing Moon   Moon Phase: Second Quarter
Color: Red

☿ **July 28**

Independence Day (Peruvian)   Moon Sign: Sagittarius
Waxing Moon   Moon Phase: Second Quarter
Color: Topaz   Moon enters Capricorn 11:57 pm

♃ **July 29**

Pardon of the Birds (French)   Moon Sign: Capricorn
Waxing Moon   Moon Phase: Second Quarter
Color: Turquoise

♀ **July 30**

Micmac Festival of St. Ann   Moon Sign: Capricorn
Waxing Moon   Moon Phase: Second Quarter
Color: Rose   Moon enters Aquarius 11:54 pm

♄ **July 31**

Weighing of the Aga Khan   Moon Sign: Aquarius
Waxing Moon   Moon Phase: Full Moon 2:05 pm
Color: Gray

News Item

Knights Templar Use Modern Technology to Find the Grail

A group of Scottish Knights Templar have begun to apply modern technology to an ancient mystery. Led by John Ritchie, the group is using ultrasound and thermal imagery to perform a noninvasive exploration of the area twenty feet beneath Rosslyn Chapel in a search for evidence of the Holy Grail. Rosslyn Chapel is near Edinburgh, Scotland, and is rumored to possess secret underground vaults that may contain treasures, such as the Grail and even, some say, the mummified head of Jesus. Interest is high among locals eager to see if the results solve the five-centuries-old puzzle of what may be hidden under the chapel. But chances are what is found may simply raise more questions.

August 2004

August 1   ☉

Sunday

Lammas   Moon Sign: Aquarius
Waning Moon   Moon Phase: Third Quarter
Color: Orange

☽   **August 2**

Porcingula (Native American)   Moon Sign: Aquarius
Waning Moon   Moon Phase: Third Quarter
Color: Lavender   Moon enters Pisces 12:34 am

Monday

♂   **August 3**

Drimes (Greek)   Moon Sign: Pisces
Waning Moon   Moon Phase: Third Quarter
Color: Black

Tuesday

☿   **August 4**

Cook Islands Constitution Celebration   Moon Sign: Pisces
Waning Moon   Moon Phase: Third Quarter
Color: Yellow   Moon enters Aries 3:59 am

Wednesday

♃   **August 5**

Benediction of the Sea (French)   Moon Sign: Aries
Waning Moon   Moon Phase: Third Quarter
Color: Crimson

Thursday

♀   **August 6**

Hiroshima Peace Ceremony   Moon Sign: Aries
Waning Moon   Moon Phase: Third Quarter
Color: Purple   Moon enters Taurus 11:26 am

Friday

♄   **August 7**

Republic Day (Ivory Coast)   Moon Sign: Taurus
Waning Moon   Moon Phase: Fourth Quarter 6:01 pm
Color: Brown

Saturday

☉   **August 8**

Dog Days (Japanese)   Moon Sign: Taurus
Waning Moon   Moon Phase: Fourth Quarter
Color: Amber   Moon enters Gemini 10:33 pm

Sunday

August 9
Monday

☽

Nagasaki Peace Ceremony
Waning Moon
Color: White

Moon Sign: Gemini
Moon Phase: Fourth Quarter

August 10
Tuesday

♂

St. Lawrence's Day
Waning Moon
Color: Gray

Moon Sign: Gemini
Moon Phase: Fourth Quarter

August 11
Wednesday

☿

Puck Fair (Irish)
Waning Moon
Color: Topaz

Moon Sign: Gemini
Moon Phase: Fourth Quarter
Moon enters Cancer 11:20 am

August 12
Thursday

♃

Fiesta of Santa Clara
Waning Moon
Color: Green

Moon Sign: Cancer
Moon Phase: Fourth Quarter

August 13
Friday

♀

Women's Day (Tunisian)
Waning Moon
Color: Rose

Moon Sign: Cancer
Moon Phase: Fourth Quarter
Moon enters Leo 11:30 pm

August 14
Saturday

♄

Festival at Sassari
Waning Moon
Color: Blue

Moon Sign: Leo
Moon Phase: Fourth Quarter

August 15
Sunday

☉

Assumption Day
Waning Moon
Color: Yellow

Moon Sign: Leo
Moon Phase: New Moon 9:24 pm

☽

August 16

Festival of Minstrels (European)
Waxing Moon
Color: Silver

Moon Sign: Leo
Moon Phase: First Quarter
Moon enters Virgo 9:49 am

♂

August 17

Feast of the Hungry Ghosts (Chinese)
Waxing Moon
Color: White

Moon Sign: Virgo
Moon Phase: First Quarter

☿

August 18

St. Helen's Day
Waxing Moon
Color: Brown

Moon Sign: Virgo
Moon Phase: First Quarter
Moon enters Libra 6:09 pm

♃

August 19

Rustic Vinalia (Roman)
Waxing Moon
Color: Turquoise

Moon Sign: Libra
Moon Phase: First Quarter

♀

August 20

Constitution Day (Hungarian)
Waxing Moon
Color: Pink

Moon Sign: Libra
Moon Phase: First Quarter

♄

August 21

Consualia (Roman)
Waxing Moon
Color: Gray

Moon Sign: Libra
Moon Phase: First Quarter
Moon enters Scorpio 12:37 am

☉

August 22

Feast of the Queenship of Mary (English)
Waxing Moon
Color: Orange

Moon Sign: Scorpio
Moon Phase: First Quarter
Sun enters Virgo 2:53 pm

August 23 ☽

Monday

National Day (Romanian)
Waxing Moon
Color: Ivory

Moon Sign: Scorpio
Moon Phase: Second Quarter 6:12 am
Moon enters Sagittarius 5:08 am

August 24 ♂

Tuesday

St. Bartholomew's Day
Waxing Moon
Color: Scarlet

Moon Sign: Sagittarius
Moon Phase: Second Quarter

August 25 ☿

Wednesday

Feast of the Green Corn (Native American)
Waxing Moon
Color: White

Moon Sign: Sagittarius
Moon Phase: Second Quarter
Moon enters Capricorn 7:46 am

August 26 ♃

Thursday

Pardon of the Sea (French)
Waxing Moon
Color: Purple

Moon Sign: Capricorn
Moon Phase: Second Quarter

August 27 ♀

Friday

Summer Break (English)
Waxing Moon
Color: Coral

Moon Sign: Capricorn
Moon Phase: Second Quarter
Moon enters Aquarius 9:08 am

August 28 ♄

Saturday

St. Augustine's Day
Waxing Moon
Color: Indigo

Moon Sign: Aquarius
Moon Phase: Second Quarter

August 29 ☉

Sunday

St. John's Beheading
Waxing Moon
Color: Amber

Moon Sign: Aquarius
Moon Phase: Full Moon 10:22 pm
Moon enters Pisces 10:33 am

☽   **August 30**
St. Rose of Lima Day (Peruvian)   Moon Sign: Pisces
Waning Moon   Moon Phase: Third Quarter
Color: Gray

♂   **August 31**
Unto These Hills Pageant (Cherokee)   Moon Sign: Pisces
Waning Moon   Moon Phase: Third Quarter
Color: Black   Moon enters Aries 1:46 pm

News Item

Brain Misfirings May Be Cause of Out-of-Body and Near-Death Experiences

A Swiss study, published in the scientific journal *Nature*, has indicated that many reported near-death and out-of-body experiences may have a biochemical, rather than a metaphysical, cause. The study hypothesizes that when the brain misfires under stress a small part of the organ may be responsible for the brilliant white lights and floating sensations often reported and associated with the occult. While the scientists admit that their work does not explain all reported instances of these phenomena, they do feel that their research reveals a more scientific basis for events that have previously been relegated to the domain of metaphysics.

September 2004

September 1   ☿

Greek New Year
Waning Moon
Color: Brown

Moon Sign: Aries
Moon Phase: Third Quarter

September 2   ♃

St. Mamas's Day
Waning Moon
Color: Crimson

Moon Sign: Aries
Moon Phase: Third Quarter
Moon enters Taurus 8:16 pm

September 3   ♀

Founder's Day (San Marino)
Waning Moon
Color: Rose

Moon Sign: Taurus
Moon Phase: Third Quarter

September 4   ♄

Los Angeles' Birthday
Waning Moon
Color: Blue

Moon Sign: Taurus
Moon Phase: Third Quarter

September 5   ☉

First Labor Day (1882)
Waning Moon
Color: Yellow

Moon Sign: Taurus
Moon Phase: Fourth Quarter
Moon enters Gemini 6:24 am

☽   September 6

Labor Day (observed)

Moon Sign: Gemini

Waning Moon

Moon Phase: Fourth Quarter 11:10 am

Color: Lavender

♂   September 7

Festival of the Durga (Hindu)

Moon Sign: Gemini

Waning Moon

Moon Phase: Fourth Quarter

Color: Red

Moon enters Cancer 6:40 pm

☿   September 8

Birthday of the Virgin Mary

Moon Sign: Cancer

Waning Moon

Moon Phase: Fourth Quarter

Color: White

♃   September 9

Chrysanthemum Festival (Japanese)

Moon Sign: Cancer

Waning Moon

Moon Phase: Fourth Quarter

Color: Green

♀   September 10

Festival of the Poets (Japanese)

Moon Sign: Cancer

Waning Moon

Moon Phase: Fourth Quarter

Color: Pink

Moon enters Leo 7:06 am

♄   September 11

Coptic New Year

Moon Sign: Leo

Waning Moon

Moon Phase: Fourth Quarter

Color: Brown

☉   September 12

National Day (Ethiopian)

Moon Sign: Leo

Waning Moon

Moon Phase: Fourth Quarter

Color: Orange

Moon enters Virgo 5:16 pm

September 13 ☽

The Gods' Banquet (Roman)
Waning Moon
Color: Silver

Moon Sign: Virgo
Moon Phase: Fourth Quarter

September 14 ♂

Holy Cross Day
Waning Moon
Color: White

Moon Sign: Virgo
Moon Phase: New Moon 10:29 am

September 15 ☿

Birthday of the Moon (Chinese)
Waxing Moon
Color: Topaz

Moon Sign: Virgo
Moon Phase: First Quarter
Moon enters Libra 12:54 am

September 16 ♃

Rosh Hashanah
Waxing Moon
Color: Turquoise

Moon Sign: Libra
Moon Phase: First Quarter

September 17 ♀

Von Steuben's Day
Waxing Moon
Color: Purple

Moon Sign: Libra
Moon Phase: First Quarter
Moon enters Scorpio 6:25 am

September 18 ♄

Dr. Johnson's Birthday
Waxing Moon
Color: Gray

Moon Sign: Scorpio
Moon Phase: First Quarter

September 19 ☉

St. Januarius' Day (Italian)
Waxing Moon
Color: Amber

Moon Sign: Scorpio
Moon Phase: First Quarter
Moon enters Sagittarius 10:30 am

☽ September 20

St. Eustace's Day
Waxing Moon
Color: Ivory

Moon Sign: Sagittarius
Moon Phase: First Quarter

♂ September 21

Christ's Hospital Founder's Day (British)
Waxing Moon
Color: Black

Moon Sign: Sagittarius
Moon Phase: Second Quarter 11:54 am
Moon enters Capricorn 1:35 pm

☿ September 22

Mabon · Fall Equinox
Waxing Moon
Color: Yellow

Moon Sign: Capricorn
Moon Phase: Second Quarter
Sun enters Libra 12:30 pm

♃ September 23

Shubun no Hi (Chinese)
Waxing Moon
Color: Purple

Moon Sign: Capricorn
Moon Phase: Second Quarter
Moon enters Aquarius 4:10 pm

♀ September 24

Schwenkenfelder Thanksgiving (Germ.-American)
Waxing Moon
Color: White

Moon Sign: Aquarius
Moon Phase: Second Quarter

♄ September 25

Yom Kippur
Waxing Moon
Color: Blue

Moon Sign: Aquarius
Moon Phase: Second Quarter
Moon enters Pisces 6:55pm

☉ September 26

Feast of Santa Justina (Mexican)
Waxing Moon
Color: Gold

Moon Sign: Pisces
Moon Phase: Second Quarter

Monday

September 27 ☽

Saints Cosmas and Damian's Day
Waxing Moon
Color: Gray

Moon Sign: Pisces
Moon Phase: Second Quarter
Moon enters Aries 10:57 pm

Tuesday

September 28 ♂

Confucius' Birthday
Waxing Moon
Color: Maroon

Moon Sign: Aries
Moon Phase: Full Moon 9:09 am

Wednesday

September 29 ☿

Michaelmas
Waning Moon
Color: Brown

Moon Sign: Aries
Moon Phase: Third Quarter

Thursday

September 30 ♃

Sukkot begins
Waning Moon
Color: White

Moon Sign: Aries
Moon Phase: Third Quarter
Moon enters Taurus 5:24 am

News Item

Floating Chapel Embraces All Creeds

The chapel aboard aircraft carrier USS *Abraham Lincoln* is a drab room flanked by steam pipes. The deafening roar of jets taking off and landing fills the air. Yet it is here, with folding metal chairs, that Navy sailors of different creeds can find time for their spirituality. You might find a Wiccan meditation circle, Catholics at confession, Muslims with prayer rugs, or Jewish Sabbath observations. The military makes every effort to allow those in uniform the opportunity to practice religious beliefs as best as circumstances will allow.

October 2004

♀   **October 1**
Armed Forces Day (South Korean)   Moon Sign: Taurus
Waning Moon   Moon Phase: Third Quarter
Color: Pink   Moon enters Capricorn 10:21 pm

Friday

♄   **October 2**
Old Man's Day (Virgin Islands)   Moon Sign: Taurus
Waning Moon   Moon Phase: Third Quarter
Color: Indigo   Moon enters Gemini 2:55 pm

Saturday

☉   **October 3**
Moroccan New Year's Day   Moon Sign: Gemini
Waning Moon   Moon Phase: Third Quarter
Color: Orange

Sunday

October 4

St. Francis' Day
Waning Moon
Color: Silver

☽

Moon Sign: Gemini
Moon Phase: Third Quarter

October 5

Republic Day (Portuguese)
Waning Moon
Color: Black

♂

Moon Sign: Gemini
Moon Phase: Third Quarter
Moon enters Cancer 2:54 am

October 6

Sukkot ends
Waning Moon
Color: Yellow

☿

Moon Sign: Cancer
Moon Phase: Fourth Quarter 6:12 am

October 7

Kermesse (German)
Waning Moon
Color: Turquoise

♃

Moon Sign: Cancer
Moon Phase: Fourth Quarter
Moon enters Leo 3:23 pm

October 8

Okunchi (Japanese)
Waning Moon
Color: Coral

♀

Moon Sign: Leo
Moon Phase: Fourth Quarter

October 9

Alphabet Day (South Korean)
Waning Moon
Color: Blue

♄

Moon Sign: Leo
Moon Phase: Fourth Quarter

October 10

Health Day (Japanese)
Waning Moon
Color: Gold

☉

Moon Sign: Leo
Moon Phase: Fourth Quarter
Moon enters Virgo 2:00 am

☽ October 11

Columbus Day (observed)
Waning Moon
Color: Ivory

Moon Sign: Virgo
Moon Phase: Fourth Quarter

♂ October 12

National Day (Spanish)
Waning Moon
Color: Red

Moon Sign: Virgo
Moon Phase: Fourth Quarter
Moon enters Libra 9:32 am

☿ October 13

Fontinalia (Roman)
Waning Moon
Color: Brown

Moon Sign: Libra
Moon Phase: New Moon 10:48 pm

♃ October 14

Battle Festival (Japan)
Waxing Moon
Color: Purple

Moon Sign: Libra
Moon Phase: First Quarter
Moon enters Scorpio 2:10 pm

♀ October 15

Ramadan begins
Waxing Moon
Color: Rose

Moon Sign: Scorpio
Moon Phase: First Quarter

♄ October 16

The Lion Sermon (British)
Waxing Moon
Color: Black

Moon Sign: Scorpio
Moon Phase: First Quarter
Moon enters Sagittarius 4:58 pm

☉ October 17

Pilgrimage to Paray-le-Monial
Waxing Moon
Color: Yellow

Moon Sign: Sagittarius
Moon Phase: First Quarter

October 18
Monday ☽

Brooklyn Barbecue
Waxing Moon
Color: Gray

Moon Sign: Sagittarius
Moon Phase: First Quarter
Moon enters Capricorn 7:07 pm

October 19
Tuesday ♂

Our Lord of Miracles Procession (Peruvian)
Waxing Moon
Color: Maroon

Moon Sign: Capricorn
Moon Phase: First Quarter

October 20
Wednesday ☿

Colchester Oyster Feast
Waxing Moon
Color: White

Moon Sign: Capricorn
Moon Phase: Second Quarter 5:59 pm
Moon enters Aquarius 9:38 pm

October 21
Thursday ♃

Feast of the Black Christ
Waxing Moon
Color: Green

Moon Sign: Aquarius
Moon Phase: Second Quarter

October 22
Friday ♀

Goddess of Mercy Day (Chinese)
Waxing Moon
Color: Purple

Moon Sign: Aquarius
Moon Phase: Second Quarter
Sun enters Scorpio 9:49 pm

October 23
Saturday ♄

Revolution Day (Hungarian)
Waxing Moon
Color: Brown

Moon Sign: Aquarius
Moon Phase: Second Quarter
Moon enters Pisces 1:13 am

October 24
Sunday ☉

United Nations Day
Waxing Moon
Color: Amber

Moon Sign: Pisces
Moon Phase: Second Quarter

☽ October 25

St. Crispin's Day
Waxing Moon
Color: Lavender

Moon Sign: Pisces
Moon Phase: Second Quarter
Moon enters Aries 6:24 am

♂ October 26

Quit Rent Ceremony (British)
Waxing Moon
Color: White

Moon Sign: Aries
Moon Phase: Second Quarter

☿ October 27

Feast of the Holy Souls
Waxing Moon
Color: Topaz

Moon Sign: Aries
Moon Phase: Full Moon 11:07 pm
Moon enters Taurus 1:37 pm

♃ October 28

Ochi Day (Greek)
Waning Moon
Color: Crimson

Moon Sign: Taurus
Moon Phase: First Quarter

♀ October 29

Iroquois Feast of the Dead
Waning Moon
Color: Pink

Moon Sign: Taurus
Moon Phase: Third Quarter
Moon enters Gemini 11:11 pm

♄ October 30

Meiji Festival (Japanese)
Waning Moon
Color: Gray

Moon Sign: Gemini
Moon Phase: Third Quarter

☉ October 31

Halloween · Samhain · Daylight Saving Time ends
Waning Moon
Color: Gold

Moon Sign: Gemini
Moon Phase: Third Quarter

J002E3: New Moon or Space Junk?

An amateur astronomer in Arizona recently discovered an uncatalogued small object roaming the solar system. After it was reported to the Minor Planets Center, the object was given the identification number "J002E3." Some analysts initially though the object might have been a new Earth satellite, but further analysis concluded the object is probably part of Apollo 12's third stage rocket. J002E3 has a one-in-five chance of crashing into the Moon, and an outside chance of hitting the Earth within the next ten years. The Earth already has two satellites: the Moon and a small asteroid with the Celtic tribal name "Cruithne," discovered in 1986.

Shelters Work to Keep Black Cats Safe during Samhain

Black cats have traditionally been associated with witchcraft, and never more so than at Samhain (Halloween). Animal shelters in many areas of the country have witnessed a dramatic rise in the number of black cat adoptions in the week prior to October 31, but unfortunately many of these adoptions do not last much beyond the holiday. In an effort to prevent this, many shelters now ban black cat adoptions for a week or two prior to Halloween. Some have gone so far as to extend the ban to all cats, not just black ones.

November 2004

☽

November 1

All Saints' Day
Waning Moon
Color: Silver

Moon Sign: Gemini
Moon Phase: Third Quarter
Moon enters Cancer 9:53 am

Monday

♂

November 2

All Souls' Day · Election Day
Waning Moon
Color: Black

Moon Sign: Cancer
Moon Phase: Third Quarter

Tuesday

☿

November 3

St. Hubert's Day
Waning Moon
Color: Yellow

Moon Sign: Cancer
Moon Phase: Third Quarter
Moon enters Leo 10:32 pm

Wednesday

♃

November 4

Mischief Night (British)
Waning Moon
Color: Turquoise

Moon Sign: Leo
Moon Phase: Third Quarter

Thursday

♀

November 5

Guy Fawkes Night (British)
Waning Moon
Color: White

Moon Sign: Leo
Moon Phase: Fourth Quarter 12:53 am

Friday

♄

November 6

Leonard's Ride (German)
Waning Moon
Color: Indigo

Moon Sign: Leo
Moon Phase: Fourth Quarter
Moon enters Virgo 10:00 am

Saturday

☉

November 7

Mayan Day of the Dead
Waning Moon
Color: Orange

Moon Sign: Virgo
Moon Phase: Fourth Quarter

Sunday

November 8
The Lord Mayor's Show (England)
Waning Moon
Color: Ivory

☽

Moon Sign: Virgo
Moon Phase: Fourth Quarter
Moon enters Libra 6:23 pm

November 9
Lord Mayor's Day (British)
Waning Moon
Color: Red

♂

Moon Sign: Libra
Moon Phase: Fourth Quarter

November 10
Martin Luther's Birthday
Waning Moon
Color: White

☿

Moon Sign: Libra
Moon Phase: Fourth Quarter
Moon enters Scorpio 11:05 pm

November 11
Veterans Day
Waning Moon
Color: Green

♃

Moon Sign: Scorpio
Moon Phase: Fourth Quarter

November 12
Tesuque Feast Day (Native American)
Waning Moon
Color: Coral

♀

Moon Sign: Scorpio
Moon Phase: New Moon 9:27 am

November 13
Festival of Jupiter (Roman)
Waxing Moon
Color: Blue

♄

Moon Sign: Scorpio
Moon Phase: First Quarter
Moon enters Sagittarius 12:56 am

November 14
Ramadan ends
Waxing Moon
Color: Amber

☉

Moon Sign: Sagittarius
Moon Phase: First Quarter

☽ **November 15**

St. Leopold's Day
Waxing Moon
Color: White

Moon Sign: Sagittarius
Moon Phase: First Quarter
Moon enters Capricorn 1:33 am

♂ **November 16**

St. Margaret of Scotland's Day
Waxing Moon
Color: Gray

Moon Sign: Capricorn
Moon Phase: First Quarter

☿ **November 17**

Queen Elizabeth's Day
Waxing Moon
Color: Brown

Moon Sign: Capricorn
Moon Phase: First Quarter
Moon enters Aquarius 2:39 am

♃ **November 18**

St. Plato's Day
Waxing Moon
Color: Purple

Moon Sign: Aquarius
Moon Phase: First Quarter

♀ **November 19**

Garifuna Day (Belizian)
Waxing Moon
Color: Pink

Moon Sign: Aquarius
Moon Phase: Second Quarter 12:50 am
Moon enters Pisces 5:38 am

♄ **November 20**

Commerce God Ceremony (Japanese)
Waxing Moon
Color: Black

Moon Sign: Pisces
Moon Phase: Second Quarter

☉ **November 21**

Repentance Day (German)
Waxing Moon
Color: Yellow

Moon Sign: Pisces
Moon Phase: Second Quarter
Moon enters Aries 11:11 am
Sun enters Sagittarius 6:22 pm

November 22 ☽

St. Cecilia's Day
Waxing Moon
Color: Lavender

Moon Sign: Aries
Moon Phase: Second Quarter

November 23 ♂

St. Clement's Day
Waxing Moon
Color: White

Moon Sign: Aries
Moon Phase: Second Quarter
Moon enters Taurus 7:16 pm

November 24 ☿

Feast of the Burning Lamps (Egyptian)
Waxing Moon
Color: Topaz

Moon Sign: Taurus
Moon Phase: Second Quarter

November 25 ♃

Thanksgiving Day
Waxing Moon
Color: Crimson

Moon Sign: Taurus
Moon Phase: Second Quarter

November 26 ♀

Festival of Lights (Tibetan)
Waxing Moon
Color: Purple

Moon Sign: Taurus
Moon Phase: Full Moon 3:07 pm
Moon enters Gemini 5:25 am

November 27 ♄

St. Maximus's Day
Waning Moon
Color: Brown

Moon Sign: Gemini
Moon Phase: Third Quarter

November 28 ☉

Day of the New Dance (Tibetan)
Waning Moon
Color: Gold

Moon Sign: Gemini
Moon Phase: Third Quarter
Moon enters Cancer 5:10 pm

☽

November 29

Tubman's Birthday (Liberian)

Moon Sign: Cancer

Waning Moon

Moon Phase: Third Quarter

Color: Gray

Monday

♂

November 30

St. Andrew's Day

Moon Sign: Cancer

Waning Moon

Moon Phase: Third Quarter

Color: Maroon

Tuesday

News Item

Cable Networks Air Occult-themed Reality Game Shows

Two cable networks—VH1 and the SciFi Channel—are each planning to air occult-themed reality TV series as part of their regular programming schedules. VH1 has bought the rights to a show called "Witchcraft," based on a concept that has done well in ratings overseas. "Witchcraft" would feature twelve students who study various lessons of the craft, with one student eliminated at the end of each episode. SciFi's program is called "Mad Mad House" and features a house, called Alt Manor, where people with alternative lifestyles live and compete to be the last person left in the house. Casting calls for the show asked for "Wiccans, vampires, Trekkers, witch doctors, 'modern primitives,' yogi masters," and the like.

December 2004

December 1 ☿

Big Tea Party (Japanese)
Waning Moon
Color: Yellow

Moon Sign: Cancer
Moon Phase: Third Quarter
Moon enters Leo 5:50 am

December 2 ♃

Republic Day (Laotian)
Waning Moon
Color: Green

Moon Sign: Leo
Moon Phase: Third Quarter

December 3 ♀

St. Francis Xavier's Day
Waning Moon
Color: Pink

Moon Sign: Leo
Moon Phase: Third Quarter
Moon enters Virgo 6:00 pm

December 4 ♄

St. Barbara's Day
Waning Moon
Color: Blue

Moon Sign: Virgo
Moon Phase: Fourth Quarter 7:53 pm

December 5 ☉

Eve of St. Nicholas' Day
Waning Moon
Color: Orange

Moon Sign: Virgo
Moon Phase: Fourth Quarter

☽ **December 6**

St. Nicholas' Day
Waning Moon
Color: White

Moon Sign: Virgo
Moon Phase: Fourth Quarter
Moon enters Libra 3:46 am

♂ **December 7**

Burning the Devil (Guatemalan)
Waning Moon
Color: Black

Moon Sign: Libra
Moon Phase: Fourth Quarter

☿ **December 8**

Hanukkah begins
Waning Moon
Color: Topaz

Moon Sign: Libra
Moon Phase: Fourth Quarter
Moon enters Scorpio 9:43 am

♃ **December 9**

St. Leocadia's Day
Waning Moon
Color: Turquoise

Moon Sign: Scorpio
Moon Phase: Fourth Quarter

♀ **December 10**

Nobel Day
Waning Moon
Color: Rose

Moon Sign: Scorpio
Moon Phase: Fourth Quarter
Moon enters Sagittarius 11:54 am

♄ **December 11**

Pilgrimmage at Tortugas
Waning Moon
Color: Indigo

Moon Sign: Sagittarius
Moon Phase: New Moon 8:29 pm

☉ **December 12**

Fiesta of Our Lady of Guadalupe
Waxing Moon
Color: Yellow

Moon Sign: Sagittarius
Moon Phase: First Quarter
Sun enters Capricorn 11:42 am

December 13 ☽

St. Lucy's Day (Swedish)
Waxing Moon
Color: Silver

Moon Sign: Capricorn
Moon Phase: First Quarter

December 14 ♂

Warrior's Memorial (Japanese)
Waxing Moon
Color: Red

Moon Sign: Capricorn
Moon Phase: First Quarter
Moon enters Aquarius 11:10 am

December 15 ☿

Hanukkah ends
Waxing Moon
Color: Brown

Moon Sign: Aquarius
Moon Phase: First Quarter

December 16 ♃

Posadas (Mexican)
Waxing Moon
Color: Purple

Moon Sign: Aquarius
Moon Phase: First Quarter
Moon enters Pisces 12:24 pm

December 17 ♀

Saturnalia (Roman)
Waxing Moon
Color: White

Moon Sign: Pisces
Moon Phase: First Quarter

December 18 ♄

Feast of the Virgin of Solitude
Waxing Moon
Color: Brown

Moon Sign: Pisces
Moon Phase: Second Quarter 11:40 am
Moon enters Aries 4:52 pm

December 19 ☉

Opalia (Roman)
Waxing Moon
Color: Amber

Moon Sign: Aries
Moon Phase: Second Quarter

☽   **December 20**

Commerce God Festival   Moon Sign: Aries
Waxing Moon   Moon Phase: Second Quarter
Color: Ivory

♂   **December 21**

Yule · Winter Solstice   Moon Sign: Aries
Waxing Moon   Moon Phase: Second Quarter
Color: Gray   Moon enters Taurus 12:52 am
                                       Sun enters Capricorn 7:42 am

☿   **December 22**

Saints Chaeremon and Ischyrion's Day   Moon Sign: Taurus
Waxing Moon   Moon Phase: Second Quarter
Color: White

♃   **December 23**

Larentalia (Roman)   Moon Sign: Taurus
Waxing Moon   Moon Phase: Second Quarter
Color: Crimson   Moon enter Gemini 11:32 am

♀   **December 24**

Christmas Eve   Moon Sign: Gemini
Waxing Moon   Moon Phase: Second Quarter
Color: Coral

♄   **December 25**

Christmas   Moon Sign: Gemini
Waxing Moon   Moon Phase: Second Quarter
Color: Blue   Moon enters Cancer 11:38 pm

☉   **December 26**

Kwanzaa begins   Moon Sign: Cancer
Waxing Moon   Moon Phase: Full Moon 10:06 am
Color: Gold

December 27

Boar's Head Supper (English)
Waning Moon
Color: Lavender

☽

Moon Sign: Cancer
Moon Phase: Third Quarter

December 28

Holy Innocents' Day
Waning Moon
Color: White

♂

Moon Sign: Cancer
Moon Phase: Third Quarter
Moon enter Leo 12:14 pm

December 29

St. Thomas à Becket's Day
Waning Moon
Color: Topaz

☿

Moon Sign: Leo
Moon Phase: Third Quarter

December 30

Republic Day (Madagascar)
Waning Moon
Color: Green

♃

Moon Sign: Leo
Moon Phase: Third Quarter

December 31

New Year's Eve
Waning Moon
Color: Purple

♀

Moon Sign: Leo
Moon Phase: Third Quarter
Moon enters Virgo 12:33 am

Thai Drug Wars Increase Demand for Magic Amulets

Thailand's efforts to crack down on drug use has led to an increase in demand for magical amulets—particularly those said to protect the wearer from bullets or physical harm. Metal or clay amulets, often with Buddhist symbolism, are common in Thai culture, but some drug dealers are paying up to ten million baht (about $232,000) for a single amulet made by highly revered spiritual leaders whose charms have demonstrated a history of protection. When not used for protective purposes, these amulets can also be bought and sold on the underground market as a means of laundering money.

January 2005

♄	January 1
New Year's Day · Kwanzaa ends	Moon Sign: Virgo
Waning Moon	Moon Phase: Third Quarter
Color: Black	

Saturday

☉	January 2
First Writing (Japanese)	Moon Sign: Virgo
Waning Moon	Moon Phase: Third Quarter
Color: Yellow	Moon enter Libra 11:19 am

Sunday

January 3 ☽

Monday

St. Genevieve's Day
Waning Moon
Color: Gray

Moon Sign: Libra
Moon Phase: Fourth Quarter 12:46 pm

January 4 ♂

Tuesday

Frost Fairs on the Thames
Waning Moon
Color: Red

Moon Sign: Libra
Moon Phase: Fourth Quarter
Moon enter Scorpio 7:00 pm

January 5 ☿

Wednesday

Epiphany Eve
Waning Moon
Color: Brown

Moon Sign: Scorpio
Moon Phase: Fourth Quarter

January 6 ♃

Thursday

Epiphany
Waning Moon
Color: Green

Moon Sign: Scorpio
Moon Phase: Fourth Quarter
Moon enters Sagittarius 10:44 pm

January 7 ♀

Friday

Rizdvo (Ukrainian)
Waning Moon
Color: White

Moon Sign: Sagittarius
Moon Phase: Fourth Quarter

January 8 ♄

Saturday

Midwives' Day
Waning Moon
Color: Indigo

Moon Sign: Sagittariu
Moon Phase: Fourth Quarter
Moon enters Capricorn 11:11 pm

January 9 ☉

Sunday

Feast of the Black Nazarene (Filipino)
Waning Moon
Color: Orange

Moon Sign: Capricorn
Moon Phase: Fourth Quarter

☽

January 10

Business God's Day (Japanese)
Waning Moon
Color: Lavender

Moon Sign: Capricorn
Moon Phase: New Moon 7:03 am
Moon enters Aquarius 10:07 pm

♂

January 11

Carmentalia (Roman)
Waxing Moon
Color: Black

Moon Sign: Aquarius
Moon Phase: First Quarter

☿

January 12

Revolution Day (Tanzanian)
Waxing Moon
Color: White

Moon Sign: Aquarius
Moon Phase: First Quarter
Moon enters Pisces 9:50 pm

♃

January 13

Twentieth Day (Norwegian)
Waxing Moon
Color: Turquoise

Moon Sign: Pisces
Moon Phase: First Quarter

♀

January 14

Feast of the Ass (French)
Waxing Moon
Color: Pink

Moon Sign: Pisces
Moon Phase: First Quarter

♄

January 15

Martin Luther King Jr.'s Birthday (actual)
Waxing Moon
Color: Gray

Moon Sign: Pisces
Moon Phase: First Quarter
Moon enters Aries 12:27 am

☉

January 16

Apprentices' Day
Waxing Moon
Color: Gold

Moon Sign: Aries
Moon Phase: First Quarter

January 17

Birthday of Martin Luther King, Jr. (observed)　　　Moon Sign: Aries
Waxing Moon　　　　　　Moon Phase: Second Quarter 1:57 am
Color: White　　　　　　　　　　　Moon enters Taurus 7:06 am

☽

January 18

Assumption Day　　　　　　　　　　Moon Sign: Taurus
Waxing Moon　　　　　　Moon Phase: Second Quarter
Color: Maroon

♂

January 19

Sun enters Aquarius　　　　　　　　Moon Sign: Taurus
Waxing Moon　　　　　　Moon Phase: Second Quarter
Color: Yellow　　　　　　　　　Moon enters Gemini 5:24 pm
　　　　　　　　　　　　　　Sun enters Aquarius 6:22 pm

☿

January 20

Inauguration Day　　　　　　　　　Moon Sign: Gemini
Waxing Moon　　　　　　Moon Phase: Second Quarter
Color: Purple

♃

January 21

St. Agnes Day　　　　　　　　　　Moon Sign: Gemini
Waxing Moon　　　　　　Moon Phase: Second Quarter
Color: Rose

♀

January 22

Saint Vincent's Day　　　　　　　　Moon Sign: Gemini
Waxing Moon　　　　　　Moon Phase: Second Quarter
Color: Black　　　　　　　　　Moon enters Cancer 5:42 am

♄

January 23

St. Ildefonso's Day　　　　　　　　Moon Sign: Cancer
Waxing Moon　　　　　　Moon Phase: Second Quarter
Color: Amber

☉

☽ January 24

Alasitas Fair (Bolivian)
Waxing Moon
Color: Silver

Moon Sign: Cancer
Moon Phase: Second Quarter
Moon enters Leo 6:21 pm

♂ January 25

Burns' Night (Scottish)
Waxing Moon
Color: Scarlet

Moon Sign: Leo
Moon Phase: Full Moon 5:32 am

☿ January 26

Republic Day (Indian)
Waning Moon
Color: Topaz

Moon Sign: Leo
Moon Phase: Third Quarter

♃ January 27

Vogelgruff (Swiss)
Waning Moon
Color: White

Moon Sign: Leo
Moon Phase: Third Quarter
Moon enters Virgo 6:24 am

♀ January 28

St. Charlemagne's Day
Waning Moon
Color: Coral

Moon Sign: Virgo
Moon Phase: Third Quarter

♄ January 29

Australia Day
Waning Moon
Color: Blue

Moon Sign: Virgo
Moon Phase: Third Quarter
Moon enters Libra 5:13 pm

☉ January 30

Three Hierarch's Day (Eastern Orthodox)
Waning Moon
Color: Orange

Moon Sign: Libra
Moon Phase: Third Quarter

January 31

Independence Day (Nauru)
Waning Moon
Color: Ivory

☽

Moon Sign: Libra
Moon Phase: Third Quarter

——— February 2005 ———

February 1

St. Brigid's Day (Irish)
Waning Moon
Color: Black

♂

Moon Sign: Libra
Moon Phase: Third Quarter
Moon enters Scorpio 1:51 am

February 2

Imbolc · Groundhog Day
Waning Moon
Color: Brown

☿

Moon Sign: Scorpio
Moon Phase: Fourth Quarter 2:27 am

February 3

St. Blaise's Day
Waning Moon
Color: Green

♃

Moon Sign: Scorpio
Moon Phase: Fourth Quarter
Moon enters Sagittarius 7:21 am

February 4

Independence Day (Sri Lankan)
Waning Moon
Color: Pink

♀

Moon Sign: Sagittarius
Moon Phase: Fourth Quarter

February 5

Festival de la Alcaldesa (Italian)
Waning Moon
Color: Gray

♄

Moon Sign: Sagittarius
Moon Phase: Fourth Quarter
Moon enters Capricorn 9:32 am

February 6

Bob Marley's Birthday (Jamaica)
Waning Moon
Color: Orange

☉

Moon Sign: Capricorn
Moon Phase: Fourth Quarter

☽ **February 7**

Saint Richard's Day (English)
Waning Moon
Color: Lavender

Moon Sign: Capricorn
Moon Phase: Fourth Quarter
Moon enters Aquarius 9:26 am

♂ **February 8**

Mardi Gras · Mass for Broken Needles (Japanese)
Waning Moon
Color: Maroon

Moon Sign: Aquarius
Moon Phase: New Moon 5:28 pm

☿ **February 9**

Chinese New Year (rooster) · Ash Wednesday
Waxing Moon
Color: Yellow

Moon Sign: Aquarius
Moon Phase: First Quarter
Moon enters Pisces 8:59 am

♃ **February 10**

Gasparilla Day (Florida)
Waxing Moon
Color: White

Moon Sign: Pisces
Moon Phase: First Quarter

♀ **February 11**

Foundation Day (Japanese)
Waxing Moon
Color: Rose

Moon Sign: Pisces
Moon Phase: First Quarter
Moon enters Aries 10:21 am

♄ **February 12**

Lincoln's Birthday (actual)
Waxing Moon
Color: Brown

Moon Sign: Aries
Moon Phase: First Quarter

☉ **February 13**

Parentalia (Roman)
Waxing Moon
Color: Gold

Moon Sign: Aries
Moon Phase: First Quarter
Moon enters Taurus 3:18 pm

February 14

Valentine's Day
Waxing Moon
Color: Silver

Moon Sign: Taurus
Moon Phase: First Quarter

☽

February 15

Lupercalia (Roman)
Waxing Moon
Color: Gray

Moon Sign: Taurus
Moon Phase: Second Quarter 7:16 pm

♂

February 16

Fumi-e (Japanese)
Waxing Moon
Color: White

Moon Sign: Taurus
Moon Phase: Second Quarter
Moon enters Gemini 12:18 am

☿

February 17

Quirinalia (Roman)
Waxing Moon
Color: Turquoise

Moon Sign: Gemini
Moon Phase: Second Quarter

♃

February 18

Saint Bernadette's Second Vision
Waxing Moon
Color: Coral

Moon Sign: Gemini
Moon Phase: Second Quarter
Moon enters Cancer 12:13 pm

♀

February 19

Pero Palo's Trial (Spanish)
Waxing Moon
Color: Blue

Moon Sign: Cancer
Moon Phase: Second Quarter

♄

February 20

Installation of the New Lama (Tibetan)
Waxing Moon
Color: Yellow

Moon Sign: Cancer
Moon Phase: Second Quarter

☉

☽ **February 21**

President's Day (observed)
Waxing Moon
Color: Ivory

Moon Sign: Cancer
Moon Phase: Second Quarter
Moon enters Leo 12:54 am

♂ **February 22**

Caristia (Roman)
Waxing Moon
Color: Scarlet

Moon Sign: Leo
Moon Phase: Second Quarter

☿ **February 23**

Terminalia (Roman)
Waxing Moon
Color: Topaz

Moon Sign: Leo
Moon Phase: Full Moon 11:54 pm
Moon enters Virgo 12:44 pm

♃ **February 24**

Regifugium (Roman)
Waning Moon
Color: Purple

Moon Sign: Virgo
Moon Phase: Third Quarter

♀ **February 25**

St. Walburga's Day
Waning Moon
Color: White

Moon Sign: Virgo
Moon Phase: Third Quarter
Moon enters Libra 10:59 pm

♄ **February 26**

Zamboanga Festival (Filipino)
Waning Moon
Color: Black

Moon Sign: Libra
Moon Phase: Third Quarter

☉ **February 27**

Threepenny Day
Waning Moon
Color: Amber

Moon Sign: Libra
Moon Phase: Third Quarter

February 28

☽

Kalevala (Finnish)
Waning Moon
Color: Gray

Moon Sign: Libra
Moon Phase: Third Quarter
Moon enters Scorpio 7:21 am

March 2005

March 1

♂

Matronalia (Roman)
Waning Moon
Color: Red

Moon Sign: Scorpio
Moon Phase: Third Quarter

March 2

☿

St. Chad's Day (English)
Waning Moon
Color: Yellow

Moon Sign: Scorpio
Moon Phase: Third Quarter
Moon enters Sagittarius 1:29 pm

March 3

♃

Doll Festival (Japanese)
Waning Moon
Color: Green

Moon Sign: Sagittarius
Moon Phase: Fourth Quarter 12:36 pm

March 4

♀

St. Casimir's Day (Polish)
Waning Moon
Color: Pink

Moon Sign: Sagittarius
Moon Phase: Fourth Quarter
Moon enters Capricorn 5:12 pm

March 5

♄

Isis Festival (Roman)
Waning Moon
Color: Brown

Moon Sign: Capricorn
Moon Phase: Fourth Quarter

March 6

☉

Alamo Day
Waning Moon
Color: Gold

Moon Sign: Capricorn
Moon Phase: Fourth Quarter
Moon enters Aquarius 6:49 pm

☽ **March 7**

Bird and Arbor Day
Waning Moon
Color: Lavender

Moon Sign: Aquarius
Moon Phase: Fourth Quarter

♂ **March 8**

International Women's Day
Waning Moon
Color: Black

Moon Sign: Aquarius
Moon Phase: Fourth Quarter
Moon enters Pisces 7:32 pm

☿ **March 9**

Forty Saints' Day (Romanian)
Waning Moon
Color: Brown

Moon Sign: Pisces
Moon Phase: Fourth Quarter

♃ **March 10**

Tibet Day
Waning Moon
Color: Purple

Moon Sign: Pisces
Moon Phase: New Moon 4:10 am
Moon enters Aries 9:03 pm

♀ **March 11**

Feast of Gauri (Hindu)
Waxing Moon
Color: Rose

Moon Sign: Aries
Moon Phase: First Quarter

♄ **March 12**

Receiving the Water (Buddhist)
Waxing Moon
Color: Gray

Moon Sign: Aries
Moon Phase: First Quarter

☉ **March 13**

Purification Feast (Balinese)
Waxing Moon
Color: Yellow

Moon Sign: Aries
Moon Phase: First Quarter
Moon enters Taurus 1:05 am

March 14
Monday   ☽

Mamuralia (Roman)
Waxing Moon
Color: Gray

Moon Sign: Taurus
Moon Phase: First Quarter

March 15
Tuesday   ♂

Phallus Festival (Japanese)
Waxing Moon
Color: Maroon

Moon Sign: Taurus
Moon Phase: First Quarter
Moon enters Gemini 8:44 am

March 16
Wednesday   ☿

St. Urho's Day (Finnish)
Waxing Moon
Color: White

Moon Sign: Gemini
Moon Phase: First Quarter

March 17
Thursday   ♃

St. Patrick's Day
Waxing Moon
Color: Turquoise

Moon Sign: Gemini
Moon Phase: Second Quarter 2:19 pm
Moon enters Cancer 7:44 pm

March 18
Friday   ♀

Sheelah's Day (Irish)
Waxing Moon
Color: Coral

Moon Sign: Cancer
Moon Phase: Second Quarter

March 19
Saturday   ♄

St. Joseph's Day (Sicilian)
Waxing Moon
Color: Blue

Moon Sign: Cancer
Moon Phase: Second Quarter

March 20
Sunday   ☉

Ostara · Spring Equinox · Int'l Astrology Day · Palm Sunday
Waxing Moon
Color: Amber

Moon Sign: Cancer
Moon Phase: Second Quarter
Moon enters Leo 8:17 am
Sun enters Aries 7:33 am

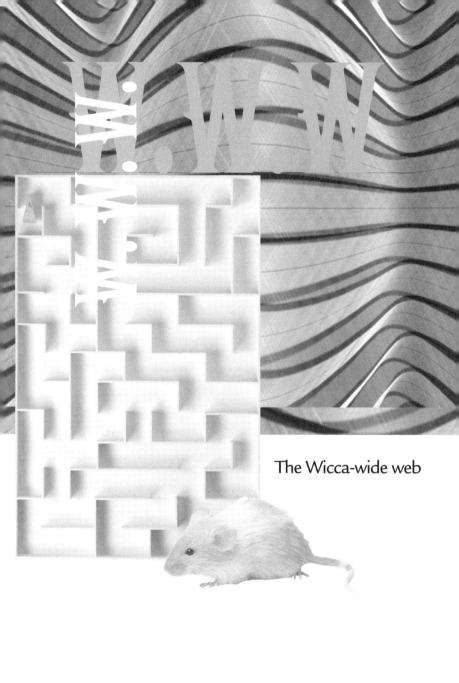

The Wicca-wide web

Navigating Pagan Chatgroups

by Boudica

The time has never been better to take an interest in the Wiccan path. There is much more information available at mainstream bookshops and at specialist New Age stores than there was just a few years ago. And then there's the Internet.

The home computer is a wonderful tool. Some of us have come to regard it as an essential part of our homescape—alongside our telephones, our TVs, and our cars. Many of us use this tool in our offices, and many of us have connections at our schools, libraries, and even coffee shops. The Internet is a whole world to explore, and Pagans have embraced it.

Personal Internet Interactions

I've been online since about 1990. I started on Prodigy back then when it cost by the hour to be on line. Now I have unlimited access, broadband, and lots of time at a minimal cost (for the most part) to explore all the avenues of contact on the web.

The ways to connect with the Pagan community on the Internet are too numerous to list, but I would like to cover some of the more well-known ways. For those of you who have never before explored the Internet, I would like to outline some basic etiquette and tips that will help make your experience a bit more "user friendly." With some assistance, what seems a complicated task can become a good, simple learning experience.

It's a good rule first off to create an online nickname for people to recognize you by. This can be fun depending on what name you choose, and it's also a matter of personal safety. Realize, though, that there are millions of people online, and that most simple nicknames will probably be in use. There are ways to make sure your name is unique, but this will require some thought and patience.

Choosing an online nickname (or *nick*) should be a simple and fun task. There are hundreds of thousands of *wolf-* or *raven-somethings,* and endless *moonthises* and *sunthats,* and you must expect that someone somewhere has already thought up your special name. One option is to use a number—"MoonBeam555,"

175

for example—to differentiate your name from similar names. Or your can use "decorations," such as OXMoonBeamXO. Just have fun with this and make yourself unique.

Always remember too that if someone else has chosen your nick before you—whether in a chat room or on an e-mail list—it's simply good policy and polite to accommodate someone who probably has been around longer than you have. I've been *Boudica* on the Internet in chat rooms, e-mail groups, and on message boards since I began in 1990. At that time there was only one other and she used a different spelling. I now have my nick registered on Undernet. But when I encounter a place where my nick is already taken, I use BoudicaCrone or boudica_. This works for me. Most of the people looking for me know my nicks and can locate me easily.

The home computer is a wonderful tool. Pagans have embraced it.

The reason for choosing a nickname is really simple: namely, security. When you start downloading programs or putting your e-mail address out there on the net, there are people who are going to want to know who you are. You really don't want anyone getting that friendly unless you know and trust them. With all the people you will encounter out on the Internet, picking and choosing who you are going to trust is a no-brainer. Begin by trusting no one, as there is no way you can get to know someone well unless you interact with them in real life. You may get friendly with some Internet denizen and may build a level of trust that could lead to real-life meetings, but above all else exercise caution when interacting on the Internet.

When downloading chat programs, exercise caution when entering personal information for registration. Same goes with setting up your personal profile on e-mail sites and in your chat profiles. You shouldn't use your real name and do not use your home e-mail address. In addition to the address you are given by your ISP, get a Yahoo or Hotmail address, or any other form of secondary e-mail address and use that one for all those forms you fill in. Think safety first. You'll save yourself much hassle from potential spammers, lurkers, and cyberstalkers. If you do find yourself receiving e-mail from someone you would rather not hear from, you can close down the secondary e-mail address and open another. It will require changing your program settings and e-mail addresses on e-mail groups, but it's better than having someone stalking you at your home e-mail address, which is not so easily changed.

One last precaution you should take is to get a good virus alert program. McAfee and Norton Antivirus are the two best on the market; both are worth the investment. You spent hundreds of dollars on your equipment; an annual investment of $40 or $50 for virus protection is rather reasonable. And always download the updates weekly to keep your machine protected. Viruses will come from e-mail, websites, and chat rooms. There is no way to filter them out without a good virus protection program.

With the safety issues out of the way, and having chosen a nick that you like and one that appears to be unique, it is time to find places to chat and communicate with others.

How to Chat on the Internet

There are several different types of chat mediums on the web. A service like AOL provides its own chat rooms. Finding Pagan chat rooms is easy; they are usually very obviously named—Pagan_Tea_House or WitchCraft. Most channels or chat rooms are open to anyone wanting to join. When you join a chat room always introduce yourself—a greeting of MM or Merry Meet is the usual form.

Avoid caplocks. Typing in all capital letters is regarded as bad manners—it indicates yelling or screaming. Type as though you are writing a letter, and you will be warmly welcomed.

The nicks of channel or chat room operators (or *ops)* are usually embellished with some kind of a symbol. These are the moderators—trusted friends who are there to oversee things. They will tell you what is going on, what code of behavior is

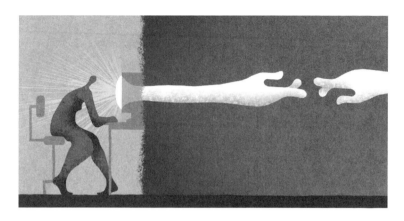

expected in that chat room, and what topics of discussion are considered appropriate. Some moderators or ops adhere strictly to channel guidelines, others are open and free for most anything you want to discuss. Be polite and adhere to the channel guidelines. If you don't like them, leave. It's very simple. The chat room belongs to whomever set it up, and their rules apply. Remember there are many channels; if one does not suit you, another will.

There are many downloadable programs for chat. mIRC is one of the most popular. While some may consider it difficult to setup, it's probably because they have been using established providers like AOL. mIRC takes minutes to set up, is relatively easy to use, costs about $20 for a lifetime of use, and offers regular free upgrades. Give it a try, and see if you like it.

mIRC is one of the oldest and most popular chat client software available and one of my personal favorites. This program gives you access to "Instant Relay Chat" (IRC) or the "Undernet," which includes many "servers" or services such as "DALnet" and "Efnet." Many of these services were started by specialty groups, such as Star Trek Fans, looking for a place to discuss their favorite shows or ideas. There was a PaganNet at one time, but the servers I have don't connect any more. The problem with a lot of Internet services is that they come and go rapidly and without much fanfare.

For those who prefer something more personal, there are severa instant messenger programs such as AIM–AOL Instant Messenger, MSN Windows Messenger, and ICQ. These are readily downloadable and easy to setup. You simply enter the nicks or IDs of the people you want to talk to, and when your friends come on line you are notified by the program so you can talk to them.

There are also "webchats" available. These are websites that provide their own chat service. They usually require some kind of download of a small java applet that automatically gives you access to their service. Yahoo provides this type of chat service with their "Yahoo Groups," and there is an IRC access without the need for mIRC software available from the "Undernet.org" site. There is no need to download any software other than their java applet, and there is hardly any setup required.

Many websites may offer a chat program in association with their site. Again, sometimes a java applet is required.

Another way to chat with other Pagans is by e-mail groups. Once called "E-Groups" because that was the name of the service, it was bought out by Yahoo a few years ago and is now called "Yahoo Groups." There is also "Topica" that provides the same type of service.

If you are like me, e-mail quantity is not a problem. However, if you don't have the time or don't want to deal with a lot of e-mail, these groups can be overpowering when it comes to the amount of e-mail you will receive on a daily basis. Depending on the activity of the group, and how many groups you belong to, you can receive a couple hundred e-mails a day. Some groups offer a "digest" option that reduces the amount of noise.

The groups are generally listed by topic. A search from the front page of the Yahoo Groups will reveal Pagan groups by tradition, by location, or by topic. Many local and national Pagan organizations maintain a Yahoo group to inform members of events and meetings. Many local Pagan groups maintain a Yahoo group to provide networking opportunities both online and in the local community. "Meet-Ups" or "Pagan Nights Outs" are the most common local community events, and when you search for a group by location you will find networking opportunities in real life. These are usually held at the local book store, coffee shop, or a comfortable restaurant. At these events, you can learn about the people who make up your group, about local events and festivals within traveling distance, about local stores, open circles, and local covens, and about other activities of interest to anyone in the Pagan Community. These are well worth the extra e-mail in your box, as there are friendships to be made out there.

Chatting does not begin and end with your computer. Your computer is a tool. Corresponding with local and national groups gives you a feel for what you may be interested in. Chatting with these people on the Internet will give you a good idea of whether or not you want to associate with these people. Meeting them in real life in public places gives you the opportunity to socialize with them and to learn if you share anything in common. Again, exercise caution. Take your time. See what the groups do, how they are organized, and what kind of characters make up the groups. Then meet members only in well-established public places. Do not accept rides from people you don't know. Just because they say they are Pagan does not mean they are any different from anyone else and should be trusted any more than any other stranger.

One more resource you may want to utilize is the "message board." These are usually found either with a provided service such AOL or on certain websites. These are reminiscent of the old BBSs (Bulletin Board Services) that were around at the beginning of the Internet, and are a place to post questions, address concerns, to rant and rave, and to get to know some members of the community.

One good example of this is the Wicca, Witchcraft and Paganism Community Forum. It is a place for book discussions, poetry, art, community notices, and other topics of interest to our community. As in all things, these boards tend to come and go. Lack of interest is usually the biggest dictator of the life expectancy of these forums, and the level of activity will tell you if it will be around for a while or if it will disappear in a few months. Some of them are fun, no matter how long they are around, and many are useful tools for learning and networking in the Pagan community.

Happy Exploring

I hope I have given you a good overview of some of the ways to reach out into the Pagan community through the Internet. Let me again emphasize that these are by no means the only ways to interact with the Pagan community, but they are good starting places if you are not well connected in your area.

The Internet should not be a substitute for personal interaction. While there are many people for whom the Internet is a major source of connection—especially for those who are physically handicapped and rarely make it out of their homes—optimally it is best to visit festivals and community events whenever you can.

I would like to list a few resources for the material I have discussed here. While the sites are still working at the time of this writing, be advised that these resources can come and go without any notice. And there will be other newer resources that may appear that I might not have mentioned.

Enjoy your Internet experience. Make it part of your life, but don't make it your whole life. And if you ever get onto IRC and find your way to the Undernet, look me up in the #zodiacbistro. I can be found there most evenings doing some networking of my own.

Resources

Please be advised that these are links to available resources, and listing them is in no way a recommendation for any specific product or website. There are so many more resources available out there and a quick search with any major search engine will give you even more choices and more resources. Feel free to explore any and all of them, but remember always to think of personal safety first.

http://www.mirc.com
mIRC Software download.

http://www.undernet.org/webchat.php
Web connection for the Undernet. After you join one of the preset channels, type in /join #channel name and you can go anywhere you want.

http://www.aim.com/
IM–AOL Instant Messenger download.

http://messenger.msn.com/
MSN download; also comes already loaded in the new Microsoft Internet Explorer package.

http://web.icq.com/
ICQ Messenger download.

http://www.aracnet.com/~avalon/cosmic/drip1.html
Humorous look at picking a Pagan name for those who need a smile

http://groups.yahoo.com/
You will need to choose a name and password if it is your first time visiting this E-group. "Chat" is also available in association with any individual e-group you join

http://www.topica.com
More E-groups.

http://www.inthemist.org/forum/
Wicca, Witchcraft, and Paganism Community Forum; message board format.

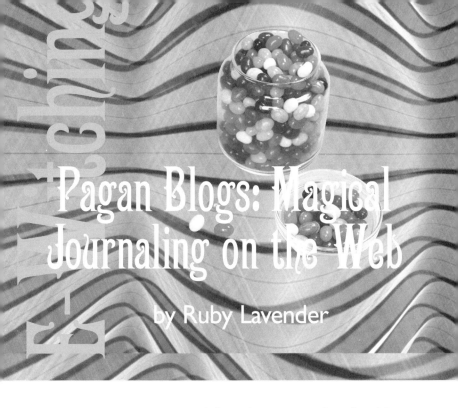

Pagan Blogs: Magical Journaling on the Web

by Ruby Lavender

You might ask, upon seeing the title to this article, "What, exactly, is a blog?" The word itself is short for "weblog," which is a personal website that is usually frequently updated to reflect events in the author's life. Some blogs read like journals or diaries; some are comprised mainly of lists of favorites things, or current literary or musical tastes, or the activities of certain people or organizations that are monitored by the "blogger," or author.

Many entries on blogs are dated so people can see how recent the information is, and for frequent readers of blogs (many of whom have their own blogs), timeliness is crucial. Blogs contain all sorts of information that is primarily of interest to the creator of the blog. But since blogs are meant to be read, these sites also are designed to provide ways for readers to interact and communicate with the authors.

Some blogs have message boards or allow commenters to post reactions to blog posts, and some blogs link to sites where this sort of interchange can take place (such as www.livejournal.com). Most blogs have the diary entries archived so new visitors can get caught up on earlier writings. Some blogs link to music, graphics, video, and other multimedia features to enhance the experience. Some bloggers select or create artwork that enhances their visuals, and often the artwork is very nicely integrated into the site. But the main feature of most blogs is the text. The experience of reading blogs is as multifaceted and various as the people who create them.

Not All Is Roses in Blog-land

A recent article on blogging in the *New York Times* described some of the problematic aspects of this practice; namely that on occasion the privacy of people whom bloggers write about may become compromised. The article also commented upon the occasional tendency of bloggers to post their diary thoughts while in the middle of an intense or heated emotional mindset, before thinking about the possible repercussions. Since most blogs contain archives of previous entries, such thoughts are often left for posterity. But that does seem to be the point: that these writers are writing to gain attention from readers who want to know about their personal experiences, thoughts, beliefs and opinions—even if they are upsetting to some.

There is a whole intricate and complex culture of blogging on the web, with sites even devoted to critiquing blogs. There are events where people blog for charitable causes (at www.blogathon.org), and various kinds of software and servers have sprung up that cater specifically to blogs. There are newsgroups and discussion lists for bloggers, and most blogs contain links to other blogs. This article is not intended to explore the whole range of blogs, which would be impossible in such a short article. Instead it is meant to introduce you to some of the Pagan blogs on the Internet.

What Is a Pagan Blog?

Many Pagans and Witches keep magical journals or diaries. One might expect a Pagan blog to be primarily magical in focus, but I found a real diversity of material in Pagan blogs. Some of the bloggers wanted to discuss their ongoing magical journey. Other Pagan bloggers prefer to

There is an intricate and complex culture of blogging on the web, with sites devoted to critiquing blogs.

have their blogs contain their own personally significant material—some of which might be Pagan or magical or occult in nature, and some not.

Pagan bloggers are like bloggers in general, in that they seem to want to give a sense of who they are to their readers, while not allowing their lives to become a literal "open book." Once upon a time, before the Internet, there was a print equivalent of the blog: the personal zine. Such self-published small magazines were sometimes little more than Xeroxed pages of someone's journal. Some were more involved—with illustrations, articles by contributors, columns, and other such features. But these zines were primarily meant to convey a highly personal worldview to anyone who might be interested in learning more about a perfect stranger's likes and dislikes, daily activities, dreams, and personal experiences.

Now that the Internet is so widely available and the print zine culture is disappearing (doubtless because websites are cheaper and easier to maintain), there has been a veritable explosion of blogging. And because the Pagan community has utilized the Internet for networking and information sharing from its humble beginnings, it was inevitable that Pagan blogs would soon become a big part of Pagan Internet culture.

Below are listed just a few of the many Pagan blogs I had a chance to look at. Blogs come and go; some last for years, with frequent updates; some go on hiatus. But one thing is for sure, new blogs will continue to appear.

Grove of the Goddess: A Seeker's Journal (http://www.avid-ity.net/magicka/)

This blog comes from Gillian Silverheart, a chronicler of magical thoughts and experiences. Though her site promises forthcoming sections on Glastonbury, Celtic gods and goddesses, the legend of King Arthur, and Celtic herbalism, most of these links are not functioning yet. But she does have articles on her experience of Goddess energy and Ireland. Once this site really gets up and running, it looks like it will appeal to many Pagans interested in the Celtic ways. I only have one suggestion for this blog: change the colors! The combinations of deep olive greens and blue are appealing, but the text and background colors do not have enough contrast and are nearly impossible to read. I look forward to reading more of this one.

Bewitching (http://mysite.verizon.net/res1l8w1/)

This is a very appealing "diary" site that is updated frequently. Each entry is preceded by a short list of qualifying statements, such as: "Subject: new CD. Time: 2:01 pm. Mood: Tranced. Music: A Dish Best Served Coldly by Type O Negative." The author likes to report what music she's listening to when composing each entry, although sometimes there is no music playing ("None right now," or "Clock ticking away.") I think this adds a fascinating personal touch, not to mention offering suggestions for my own musical exploration. The author also has a "moon tool" graphic, which gives the current phase of the Moon. Bewitching's topics range from the Pagan holidays that are occurring while she's writing, her thoughts on a new book she's read, or on activities with her family. The author also promises to repond to e-mail and questions in a timely fashion. She uses Livejournal, a website which allows people to create their own journals and where visitors can post questions. That link is: http://www.livejournal.com/users/be_witching/. The author describes her blog as: "A magical blog that contains writings about my day-to-day life as a full-time Witch, mom, and wife."

Letter from Hardscrabble Creek (http://www.chasclifton.com/blogger.html)

Chas Clifton's blog is described on his site as: "Writing on the Pagan life, with a focus on books, scholarship, and nature-based spirituality." Clifton's name is familiar to many Pagans for his books and essays. He started blogging in 2003. Recent entries include descriptions of recent travels (with photos!), reviews of books, a look at organizations like the Psychedelic Venus Church, and musings on the death of a friend. I like the fact that this scholarly Pagan has decided to craft a weblog; honestly, don't you want to know what goes on in the lives of people like this? Clifton includes links to his own books, reviews, and articles, and to those of selected favorite authors. I might have liked to see more thoughts on Clifton's involvement in academia as a Pagan, but overall this is a very interesting and focused blog.

Weblinks from the Broomcloset (http://broomcloset.pitas.com/)

This is apparently a spin-off from the an earlier site, Stories from the Broom Closet. The author, Wyrdsister, features various Pagan websites with her own brief reviews and recommendations. She also has a diary section (hosted by diaryland.com, an easy-to-use web-diary site). She links to other bloggers under a set of links called "Daily Reads," and from there I found a number of other great blogs—though not all of them are Pagan, and some are borderline (like www.easybakecoven.net, which I review below). This blogger is clearly tuned right into blog culture, and so is a great example of just how intricate and intense this experience of blogging can be for some. The author (rather courageously if you ask me) has a link where visitors can assess her blog site at a "hot or not" type site.

Easy Bake Coven (http://easybakecoven.net/)

This is a really fun blog, and despite the name I am not sure whether it is strictly Pagan or not. But since it was prominently featured in the links of a Pagan blog I'll include it here. This blog is frequently updated and has a variety of categories that will give an intimate glimpse at the interests of this writer. The blogger has several intriguing features on her site, including an archived diary, links to other blogs and music sites, and a list of current favorite interests under a series of headings that start with "Currently"—as in, "Currently reading: Kingdom of Fear," "Currently watching: Strangers With Candy," "Currently listening to: The Pretenders." It's another highly personal, idiosyncratic—but fascinating—blog feature. The blogger offers weather forecasts, news on upcoming films starring her favorite actors (like Johnny Depp, whose photo is included), and thoughts on various cultural happenings. I also enjoyed the diverse selection of "quotes for the day" from people like Alice Walker and Kahlil Gibran. You can subscribe to this blog's updates by simply entering your e-mail address—a service known as "Bloglet." Again, I was struck by the amount of blog-specific software and specially designed features that are particular to blog sites.

Myself Eternal: The Scout an Sionnach Journal (http://members.rogers.com/nuada/)

This is a simple and yet interesting site with some unusual blog features. A link that says "passion" lists the blogger's many things that "fuel my passion for life." This list includes, among many other things: "Calling a dog 'pup' . . . feeling my breath . . . nervous giggles . . . showers before bed . . . going with it . . . cloud gazing . . . electronica . . . chance meetings." The "spirit" link offers a brief exploration of how the blogger defines his spiritual path, as well as advice for other Pagan seekers. This blogger, a young Pagan from Canada, also posts a diverse sampling of diary entries of philosopical thoughts on Paganism, his various activist causes, recent books, films, and music. I liked the author's dry wit and very laid-back style of writing. Not all of the pages have links back to other areas on the site, which made navigating a bit tricky at times, but not necessarily frustrating. It is a simple, no-nonsense approach to the Pagan blog, presented by a Pagan who has a wide range of interests.

Basic Computer Magic

by Cerridwen Iris Shea

I've worked for years to learn to control my temper and live more gently without turning into a doormat. But the one thing that sends me right over the brink is an uncooperative or recalcitrant computer. To me, having a computer is a contract. I pay a sum or money to buy a device created to do certain things more efficiently than I can do them myself. I am happy to feed it and care for it as a member of my household. In return, I expect it to work—especially when I'm under deadline pressure.

The computer, of course, finds my resolve quite amusing, and thwarts me almost as soon as it's out of the box. Nothing

makes it happier than dumping the final draft of a text just before I print it. Throwing the computer out of my window would give me temporary satisfaction, but doesn't solve the problem in the long run. Plus, computer tossing gets expensive.

So I started to use magic. After all, I regularly smudge and cleanse my living space, so why shouldn't I do so with the computer? When I got my current one and set it up on my desk, I performed a smudging and naming ritual ceremony and welcomed it into my circle.

Furthermore, I keep the computer clean. I dust it, wipe the screen, the keyboards, and so on. I dilute rosemary oil and draw the runes of *Feoh, Ur,* and *Sol* (fertility, strength, and success) on its top and sides. I dilute the oil so it won't eat away at the computer's shell, and I trace the runes where I know they won't harm the computer (in other words, not on the screen!). Another friend suggested that I tape the astrological symbol for Gemini

191

to the front of the computer, since the computer is a tool for communication. However, for some reason I ended up with a computer even more psychotic than when I started.

I keep a stuffed owl on the desk for wisdom. I keep a tiger's-eye (communication), an amethyst (clarity), and a rose quartz (harmony) under the monitor as my special computer stones.

I named this computer, and I talk to it as I friend. The cats eye me rather strangely, but then, they're used to all the attention being on them. That and a three-year Come-to-My-House service warranty are working better than yelling and hitting. Although there are times, especially during Mercury retrograde, when I am rather tempted. And, yes, when I recover, I actually apologize to the computer and do another cleansing.

I don't use magic just to keep the computer up and running. I also use the computer in magical practice.

As stated before, the computer is a tool of communication. That means I can use it in work to educate, heal, and support. I can send e-mail cards and letters to friends who need help. I do research and gain inspiration for articles. I participate on message boards, and I ask for help—sometimes it's easier to ask for help from someone via an e-mail than in person.

My world expands exponentially every time I log on. I work faster than I can by hand when I'm using word-processing programs. I can even get a tarot reading online when I'm confused.

Most of all, with my computer I write spells. I receive spells. I use the energy of air (intellect) and fire (the computer runs on electricity) to bump up spells. Simply by using the computer to compose and print out spells for ritual, I add extra air and fire to the spells.

By treating the computer as a companion to my magic, instead of an obstacle to my life, I improve all areas of my life, and have an easier time walking the walk. It's not exactly a familiar, but it holds an important part in my ever-growing practice.

Over the Cauldron

Up-to-date Wiccan
opinions & rantings
overheard & spelled
out just for you

War and Peace for Pagans

by Flame RavenHawk

"You must be the change you wish to see in the world."

—Mahatma Gandhi

What is the relationship between politics and spirituality? Pagans often feel acute religious persecution, especially considering the highly politicized stance of our current president—who has expressed the view that Wicca should not be considered a religion.

In the wake of the horrible events of September 11, we can see how political divisions inform religious differences, and

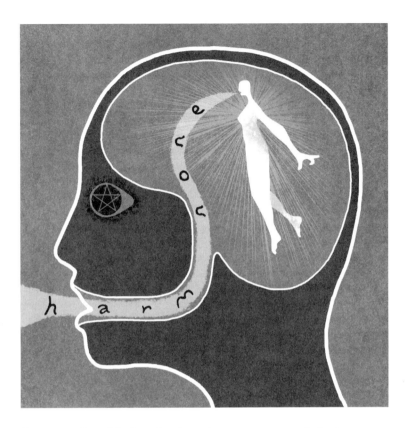

vice versa. Considering the American government's insistence on pursuing a policy of warfare in the religiously volatile Middle and Near East, it seems pointless to pretend that religion and politics don't have anything to do with each other.

Spirituality doesn't happen in a vacuum. People's spiritual and moral beliefs are influenced and impacted by events in the world around us. The recent war in Iraq, for instance, roused people in a way that hasn't been seen since Vietnam. Many Pagans opposed the war, and directly based their opposition on their spiritual beliefs. Others, remembering George W. Bush's unapologetic "born-again" fundamentalist Christianity, feel that religion should stay out of politics. The question is: Where should we draw the line between professing our Pagan beliefs and acting on those beliefs in a political world?

Walk the Talk

It isn't always easy living according to beliefs. Although Pagans revere the earth as sacred, most of us still choose the path of least resistance when it comes to many day-to-day environmental decisions. It's easier to reach for paper towels instead of reusing cloth ones. It's easier to jump into our cars than to wait for a bus. It's easier to toss a recyclable can away instead of carrying the empty around until we find a recycling bin.

On a larger scale, we face enormous challenges such as global warming, pandemic disease, overpopulation, and war. In the face of such daunting problems, it's common to allow feelings of helplessness turn to apathy and indifference. Simply put, it's easier to think that our single effort won't really matter that much, and then do nothing. Indeed, our habits often do not conform with our ideals.

Yet this is exactly what is required of us—to live according to our spiritual truths; to "walk the talk," so to speak. We're betraying our own inner sense of abiding truth when we ignore what we know to be true. And like an insidious disease, this disjunction undermines the very foundations of our deeper selves. If we do not live in harmony with what we hold to be true, then we are being false to ourselves. That is a spiritual tragedy.

Peaceful Warrior

My spirituality is a very personal thing. However, I cannot be who I am if I do not take a political stand on issues that strike directly to the core of my beliefs.

For instance, I'm a pacifist. I believe that peace should be valued and sought above all else. I am both intellectually and morally opposed to warfare as a problem-solving technique. I'm not a pacifist because I'm squeamish about the thought of death or dying. As a Wiccan, I don't have many hang-ups about death.

Rather, my political pacifism arises straight from my commitment to spiritual pursuits. As a result of a profound spiritual experience, I have seen the complete folly of war. Violence can achieve temporary results, but the violence will eventually be repaid, and no true peace can result. Peace is found through the often difficult process of seeing that everyone's needs are met.

As a pacifist, you'd think that I'd go out of my way to avoid conflict. But pacifism is a stance in regards to violence. Being a pacifist does not mean being a weakling or a sucker. It means being stronger than those who seek a quick solution through the pain, suffering, and death of others. Being a pacifist also does not mean being an idealist. In fact, to be an effective pacifist requires a profound realism and creativity in seeking peaceful solutions. Still, if my convictions aren't worth standing by, then they aren't truly convictions. And if I profess to believe in peaceful solutions, no matter how difficult they are to achieve, then I must be a constant voice for peace.

Politics: That Dirty Word

During the Iraq conflict last year, many Pagans expressed their views about war through marches, letters to their representatives, and other acts of peaceful democratic expression. Many more Pagans expressed their views in a magical way. Willow, an eclectic Pagan, expressed the unique perspective during that war.

"Why," she asked, "does 'An harm ye none' only apply to our magical lives? Why not apply it to every aspect of our lives, even if it applies to people we don't like who are doing things we don't approve of?" As a result, Willow acted in a private spiritual way to effect peace—lighting candles, praying for peace, expressing kind thoughts and giving respect to others—even as she acted politically in signing petitions, writing to political leaders, and protesting peacefully. "But I will not knowingly condone any sort of protest that can harm another regardless of whether or not I agree with them."

Again and again, we see Pagans are generally comfortable with allowing their spiritual beliefs to inform their political positions. Darkstar, who hosts the Wicca, Witchcraft, & Paganism Community Forum (http://www.inthemist.org/forum/), expressed the close bond between Pagan political and spiritual beliefs when she said: "If someone doesn't agree, they are welcome to voice an alternative opinion. I argue that, considering the impact this war will have on Mother Earth and all life on it, that it is not only a political concern, but a personal concern as well . . . We all choose to work towards a peaceful resolution to this conflict in whatever matter we see fit, and for some that includes involving our religious beliefs."

A Matter of Morals

I haven't always been so against war. I used to believe in the self-defense argument, and there might still be some rare circumstances that would slip under my low threshold for warfare.

However, it's really a very straightforward moral situation. To take another's life is deeply, morally wrong. We all generally agree on that. That's why we're so upset when someone we love is murdered. Whether you're a Christian following the commandment that "thou shalt not kill," a Buddhist following the rule of *ahimsa,* or nonviolence, or a Wiccan who believes in "harm none," we all share the common belief that taking another life is wrong.

If killing is wrong, then it is wrong for all. It can't be right for some, but not for others, or right on occasion when we think so. If we despise murderers for killing, then what makes it right when we decide to kill them? Who gave the government the higher moral authority to dispense with society's most basic beliefs?

That's why I'm opposed to killing criminals. It's been shown that the death penalty is no deterrent, especially to terrorists who are committed to martyrdom anyway. Capital punishment is state-sponsored vengeance, pure and simple. Ethically and spiri-

tually, this policy poisons us, the "punishers," because we become the very thing we condemn. Similarly, a bit of what makes this country so strong and great is eroded and poisoned when we strip away constitutional civil liberties to "protect" the land from further acts of terror. In that sense, the terrorists have won after all. We need to step past our ancient knee-jerk response to our grief and act like the strong, responsible moral leadership we claim to be to the world.

Drawing the Line

I know that mixing politics and religion isn't politically correct nowadays, but there is a place for them to mix. My basic formula is this: Since a representative government needs to represent all people, regardless of individual religious affiliation, the state should remain neutral in matters of religion. However, since religion supports an individual's system of ethical values, it should always have a place in informing our personal political decisions.

I think our spiritual pursuits should inform our stand on political issues. We must walk the talk. If we say we love Mother Earth and revere her as sacred, how can we not scream out at the governments and corporations who are killing her? If we say we believe in love and honor, how can we not speak out when we see hate and injustice? My spirituality leads me to seek the truth, so how can I help but despise the lie? And when my government lies to me—me, the citizen who grants that government authority—well, then I have a moral and legal responsibility to take action.

This might make me seem undemocratic or "unpatriotic" to some people. Several people expressed concern that I voiced my opinion so publicly. I think President Theodore Roosevelt said it best: "To announce that there must be no criticism of the president, or that we are to stand by the president, right or wrong, is not only unpatriotic and servile but is morally treasonable to the American public."

I'm comfortable with the thought that I might go against popular opinion. As a Pagan and a Witch, I have accepted that as a fundamental part of who and what I am.

Now, more than ever, we need people of conscience to pay attention to the world of politics. The prevalent American attitude to "support the flag, good or bad" is a dangerous one that releases the individual from the democratic responsibilities of citizenship. But then again, most people think of citizenship as a right, not as a responsibility. That's exactly the attitude that must change.

I think America can, and should, change its policies, because I remember that the American government was established "*by* the people, *of* the people, and *for* the people." The government exists to serve the will of the people, not the other way around. If the people lead, the leaders will follow. It may be difficult to achieve, but that is exactly what needs to happen.

We, as an American people, must stop listening to the will of the government, and insist that the government start listening to the will of the people. We must insist that our leadership stop basing their policies on the religious ethics of Christian fundamentalism, and allow each individual to express their religious freedoms—as this nation's founders intended.

> My spirituality is a very personal thing. However, I cannot be who I am if I do not take a political stand on issues that strike to the core of my beliefs.

Political change of this nature happens on the individual level. You can't change the American government from the top down. You have to educate and inform the people, because in a democracy that is where the real power is. We must ensure that our representatives are truly representing us, not special interests, and we must exercise the right that our founders were willing to die for: The right to vote and have a say in how this country is run. It is crucial that each and every American who believes in peace and in the ideals of democracy take their responsibility as a citizen more seriously.

We were given the freedom of speech for exactly this reason. I have used my voice by calling my senators, writing letters to the president, and contacting my representatives at the state and national level. I have participated in discussions in my community and online. I've written and published opinion pieces bringing this debate into the public eye. Judging by the public response, there are a lot of people out there who are tired of feeling hopeless and unempowered. The solution is simple. It's up to each one of us to do something. I encourage every voice to speak up and be heard. We are fortunate enough to live in a country that allows freedom of speech. We should use it! There are others who don't have those freedoms.

We must all speak out and say clearly and consistently that we do not want war. We, the informed public, decide public policy. If the public leads, the leaders must follow.

No effort is wasted. Each step we take as individuals to promote peace becomes part of the solution. Peace cannot be imposed from outside, and certainly it cannot be found at the point of a bullet. So keep peace and love in your heart as you firmly renounce warfare and unnecessary killing. Don't let the government's slick ad campaigns and anxiety alerts create fear in your heart. Keep peace there instead. Be a working example of peace in all that you do. From each individual heart, the peace will spread.

For Further Study

www.AlterNet.org. Excellent source for independent political news and analysis.

www.MoveOn.org. Grassroots organization "working to bring ordinary people back into politics."

www.uspirg.org. The U.S. Public Interest Research Group acts as a watchdog for public interests in the nation's capital, as well as helping to provide the grassroots organizing power necessary to influence the national policy debate.

www.FirstGov.gov. The U.S. Government's official web portal. Interact with your government!

ActionNetwork.org. An online environmental activism community that makes contacting your representatives on key environmental issues as easy as a single click of the mouse.

An' It Harm None

by Ellen Dugan

Eight words the Wiccan Rede fulfill: An' it harm none, do as you will.

I have to crane my neck to look up into the eyes of my six-foot-tall, muscle-bound, football-playing, teenage son these days. I am amazed at the volume of his voice as he insists that my request to take out the trash is unjust, unfair, and just plain mean.

"It's not my turn to take out the garbage, tonight," he informs me, for the seventh time.

I suppose he figures that if he repeats himself over and over I'll give in. At the moment I am giving serious consideration to striking him mute, right where he stands, Rede or no.

I give myself a mental shake. Teenagers must be the Goddess' way of keeping us on our ethical toes. I try to ground and center and to remind myself to not lose my temper. It lasts for about three seconds as he starts complaining again.

"You're really pushing it," I warn him, as my temper starts to unravel. I turn on the overhead lights in the kitchen, and the ceiling fan's decorative bulbs short out with a loud "pop!"

"Man," he gripes, "I really hate it when you do that!" Then he immediately backs down.

I simply smile and raise an eyebrow. "You can change those light bulbs when you come back inside." I tell him sweetly.

"I'm sorry," he gathers up the bags and looks cautiously over his shoulder at me. "I'll take out the trash."

My husband pokes his head in the kitchen, looks up and sighs. Then he grumpily mutters something about the cost of light bulbs as he goes to see if we have any replacements. I look up at the ceiling fan and blow out a relieved breath that at least I didn't trip the circuit breaker this time.

My fifteen-year-old daughter flounces into the kitchen, "Mommmm," she draws the word out with a disapproving look. "Didn't you just give me a lecture about harming none?"

"I didn't harm anybody . . ." I start to say, and then stop as she frowns at me. She is right, after all. And once again I'll have to deal with the karma of blowing up a few light bulbs. Still, when it comes to living with three teenagers, it doesn't hurt to have a good-natured bluff. After all, a mother's got to have a few tricks up her Witch's sleeve.

My son comes back into the kitchen and starts to chuckle, as his sister is still lecturing. My husband hands me the box of light bulbs and grins. I climb up on a chair. My daughter is still lecturing, my husband is still grinning, and my son is trying not to laugh at me. Finally I start to giggle and the whole family gives in as we all start to laugh at the ridiculousness of the situation.

The Rede

Wicca is a happy and loving faith. It is also a socially and ecologically responsible one. Most Witches and Wiccans delight in the natural world. They feel a spiritual connection to plants, animals, the elements, and with the people who share this Earth with us. Wiccan ethics are positive and healing. While our ethics may be summed up in a neat little phrase, they are complex and thought provoking as well. Have you ever taken a good hard look at the Wiccan Rede? Have you ever wondered where it came from or why Witches hold on to it so firmly? When was the last time you really thought about how ethics affect your magic and your life?

The Wiccan Rede is a basic tenant that all Witches learn at the beginning of their studies. This ethical consideration follows a Witch throughout training, study, and in everyday life. This familiar phrase is a neat and simple way to explain to other folks what Witches and Wiccans believe.

Where did the Rede come from? Some folks will attribute the origin of the Rede to Crowley, and his "Do what you will, is the whole of the law." Others may look to a poem, generally attributed to Doreen Valiente, which expresses the "long form" of the Witches' Creed.

Doreen Valiente is considered to be the "mother of modern Witchcraft." She wrote many of the traditional rituals, invocations, and spells that modern Witches hold dear today. This includes the poetic version of the "Charge of the Goddess," "Witches Rune," and "The Witches Creed."

But where did the Rede come from originally, and who wrote it? According to the best information, the twenty-six line Rede-poem, as we know it today, first appeared in *Green Egg* magazine (Vol. III, No. 69, Ostara, 1975) as part of an article titled "Wiccan-Pagan Potpourri."

This poem was titled "The Rede of the Wiccae" and was submitted by Lady Gwen Thompson (1928–1986). The poem was printed as Thompson's paternal grandmother, Adriana Porter, had originally given it to her. "The Rede of the Wiccae" is quite possibly the only pre-Gardnerian version of the Rede known today. Lady Gwen's lovely Rede-poem is as follows.

The Rede of the Wiccae

Bide the Wiccan laws ye must, in perfect love and perfect trust.
Live an let live, fairly take an fairly give.
Cast the circle thrice about, to keep all evil spirits out.
To bind the spell every time, let the spell be spake in rhyme.
Soft of eye and light of touch, speak little, listen much.
Deosil go by the waxing Moon, sing and dance the Wiccan rune.
Widdershins go when the Moon doth wane, an the Werewolf howls by the dread wolfsbane.
When the Lady's Moon is new, kiss the hand to her times two.
When the Moon rides her peak, then your heart's desire seek.
Heed the north wind's mighty gale, lock the door and drop the sail.
When the wind comes from the south, love will kiss thee on the mouth.
When the wind blows from the east, expect the new and set the feast.
When the west wind blow's o'er thee, departed spirits restless be.
Nine woods in the cauldron go, burn them quick an burn them slow.
Elder be the Lady's tree, burn it not or cursed ye'll be
When the Wheel begins to turn, let the Beltane fires burn.
When the wheel has turned at Yule, light the Log an let Pan rule.
Heed ye flower, bush an tree, by the Lady's blessed be.

Where the rippling waters go, cast a stone an truth ye'll know.
When ye have need, hearken not to other's greed.

With the fool no season spend, or be counted as his friend.
Merry meet and merry part, bright the cheeks and warms the
*   heart.*
Mind the threefold law ye should, three times bad an three
*   times good.*
When misfortune is enow, wear the blue star on the brow.
True in love ever be, unless thy lover's false to thee.
Eight words the Wiccan Rede fulfill, an it harm none, do
*   what ye will.*

Romantic, beautiful, and easy to read, this lengthy poem pretty much covers all of the bases. Yes, it may sound old fashioned, but it certainly is worth studying. I think the fashioned words, like "ye," only add to the charm. Could it be that we have all gotten so sure of ourselves that we feel the rules don't apply to us anymore? Ethics, kindness, beauty, and compassion do not go out of fashion. Recall the lines from the "Charge of the Goddess"—"And therefore let there be beauty and strength, power and compassion, honor and humility, mirth and reverence within you." These eight qualities are positive goals to strive for, not limiting guidelines. Meditate on these personality traits. They might be able to give you a boost in the direction that you were intended to travel all along.

The Rule of Three and Variations on a Theme

The "Witches' rule of three" has numerous variations, but the underlying message is the same, whatever you send out good or bad will return to you three times over. In other words, what goes around, comes around. So it makes no sense to work harmful or manipulative magic, since it's only going to find its way back to you in very short order.

The Rede and the Witches' rule of three are basic codes that modern Wiccans loyally adhere to. Is this a new idea? Not really. The same type of idea is held by many faiths, both mundane and magical. There are a few examples of the same type of idea. There

is the Golden Rule, "Do unto others as you would have them do unto you." The Strega, or Italian witchcraft, traditions look to the teachings of Aradia who taught her followers the "law of return"—that every magical action would draw unto itself, three times the nature of that act. Even though Aradia was not a "sweetness and light" type of deity, she did, however, encourage her followers to be responsible and to consider their actions.

There is also the Hermetic principal of cause and effect—that every action has an equal and opposite reaction. In other words, nothing happens by accident. What may seem like coincidence has a source somewhere. Every thing that you do in your life affects someone or something else. The old adage is, if you toss a pebble into the pond it will cause ripples and change the structure of the pond forever. Whatever you "toss" out there magically will return to you amplified.

The Wiccan Rede is a basic tenant that all Witches learn. It is a neat and simple way to explain to others what Wiccans believe.

As Witches and magicians we have to accept the consequences of our spells. The best way to keep your magic positive and yourself on the correct path is to embrace the tenant of harming none. Is this always easy? Nope. But it is definitely worth striving for.

We can also consider the "Nine Noble Virtues" of the Norse Pagans, the Asatru. This is the belief that actions speak louder than words. This was new information to me when I stumbled upon it. I called up a old friend who is an Asatru and picked her brain. She has these Nine Noble Virtues hanging on her refrigerator. What a great idea. In case you are unfamiliar with them, the Nine Noble Virtues are:

> *Courage—Being brave enough to do what's right.*
> *Truth—Being honest and saying what you know to be true and right.*
> *Honor—Inner value and worth; a nobility of being.*
> *Fidelity—Being loyal to the gods and goddesses, and to yourself.*
> *Discipline—To be hard on yourself first, and if need be with others; working for the greater good.*
> *Hospitality—The act of sharing what you have with others.*
> *Industriousness—Working hard is a joyous activity in itself.*
> *Self-reliance—A spirit of independence for yourself, your family, and your clan, tribe, or nation.*

Perseverance—A spirit of stick-to-it-iveness; that you perse-
vere until success is achieved.

See, the tradition doesn't matter. The basic tenants of jus-
tice, kindness, and compassion are out there, just waiting for you
to look at them with a fresh perspective.

The Rede and Real Life

Okay, you're thinking, *that's just great. What about real life and deal-*
ing with unpleasant situations or negative people? Well, my magical
friend, step up. Decide how to handle the situation, ethically,
fairly, with a little compassion and for the greater good. Recall
that you are affecting situations and other peoples lives when
you toss magic around. If you must defend yourself or your loved
ones, then do so carefully. Set aside your anger and focus on a
positive outcome to the problem. Be as conscientious as possible.
Nobody said it would be easy. With power comes responsibility.
It is your responsibility to harm none, and to set a good example.

Have you ever considered that you are a actually a role
model? Pretty scary idea, huh? Consider all the people you know.
Ask yourself how many of these people actually know other
Witches or Pagans. They probably don't know very many of
them. Guess what this means . . .

It means they judge all other Witches by you. That's right,
they look to you, and they make their judgment about Witches
in general by seeing how you conduct yourself. This makes being
a responsible Witch and ethical practitioner quite important.

So, look to the Rede and consider your actions, both magical and mundane. Then apply these enchanting principles to
your life and your magic in a whole new way. We all have to deal
with our own tempers, and when we feel threatened, or very
angry, it is difficult to remember the rules—but you must try all
the same. The law of cause-and-effect and the law of return won't
take the day off just because you're angry.

Blow off some steam before you consider magic. Take a
walk, pull some weeds, talk to a friend, or clean the house. Work

off that anger before you perform any magic. Ground and center yourself, calm down, and decide what your smartest course of action is, and then follow it.

The Most Powerful Magic

Combining magic with love and ethics is a powerful combination. Don't be afraid to love others and to laugh at yourself and at ridiculous situations in general. We all screw up from time to time; the trick is to learn from your mistakes.

Am I claiming that I have perfectly mastered these traits? Absolutely not! This is why I shared the story about my argument with my son over household duties—to show how rashly one can sometimes act.

Do your very best to be an ethical Witch and really work at setting a good example for others to follow. Like it or not, you are a role model. Be an outstanding one. Most importantly, don't forget to learn from your mistakes and magical misfirings. Move on from mistakes, and avoid repeating them. Keep a good sense of humor, because laughter and love can save the magical day.

Wiccan or Pagan, What's the Diff?

by Nancy Bennett

Here's a problem even an enlightened near-crone like me sometimes faces: I have a hard time defining who I am.

Does that happen to you too? For instance, when people ask me what kind of religion I practice I give two answers. Never mind trying to explain what kind of Witch I am, I have trouble making clear the difference between being a Pagan and being a Wiccan. I have trouble keeping them clear in my own mind. At times I wonder where the Pagan in me ends exactly, and where the Witch begins!

As a Pagan I honor and worship the Earth and the life forces in nature all around me. As a Wiccan I do all this *and* work magic—sometimes using natural forces to form my spells.

I know and understand that I am one and both things, but that does not seem to matter to the general public. Most people believe being Pagan and Wiccan is akin to being both Baptist and Catholic—that is, an impossible contradiction. So I sought out some definitions hoping this would clear it up for me and those friends and family who keep asking pesky questions.

Some Definitions

"Wicca is a gentle, Earth-oriented religion dedicated to the Goddess and God."

> Scott Cunningham, *Wicca: A Guide For the Solitary Practitioner*

"Wicca is an initiatory path, a mystery tradition that guides its initiates to a deep communion with the powers of Nature and of the human psyche, leading to a spiritual transformation of the self."

> The Pagan Federation

"Witchcraft—the practice of magic."

> *Websters Dictionary*

"Witch—A woman who practices magic and who is considered to have dealings with the devil."

> *Websters Dictionary*

"In simple terms [Paganism] is a positive, nature-based religion, preaching brotherly love and harmony with and respect for all life forms."

> Gerina Dunwich, *Wicca Craft*

"Pagan—A person who pursues his or her own vision of the divine as a direct personal experience. Paganism is the ancestral religion of humanity."

> The Pagan Federation

"Pagan—A person who has no religion. A heathen, non-Christian."

> *Websters Dictionary*

So there you have it, clear as a muddy cauldron, right? And I always was brought up to trust the dictionary as the ultimate information source!

Earth

The Collective Memory

Ever more confused, I returned to the collective memory and asked my questions of my own ancestral forebears. In the beginning of our time on this Earth wherever you looked, in whatever culture, people worshiped nature. And why not? Without nature they would not have had food to eat, air to breath, nor water to drink. They learned to take from nature for their shelters and their sustenance, and as a result they saw that nature had mysteries as well.

There were winds and rain and thundering skies. Sometimes the earth shook or in places spewed out fountains of fire and molten rivers. Sometimes snow fell and coated the land, bringing hunger and hardship. Yet other times the Sun shone and made things grow. People learned to honor the seasonal changes through ritual, and they learned to live with the Earth. These were the first Pagans.

Later, perhaps much later, priests and priestesses set about honoring deities. Perhaps these were elders who had seen many changes and were knowledgeable. Perhaps they were chosen by the people to construct rituals to pay homage to the natural forces around them. Some of these priests and priestesses took it a step farther and began to weave charms to create rituals that were intended to bring changes. They used the knowledge that they gained to guide and teach others who were like-minded. These were the first Witches.

According to Jessica, the Black Cord Witch, Witches were once considered "Pagan clergy." This was true especially of Witches who were involved in the community service aspect of the celebration of earth-based spirituality. You could be Pagan without being a Witch or Wiccan, but not the other way around. "I don't know if anyone thinks this way anymore, though," she writes. "These days, I'm inclined to think, from what I can garner of public opinion, that Witchcraft is a personal path, Wicca is an Earth-based religion that is somewhat structured, and Paganism is non-structured Earth-based spirituality."

For instance, the Pagan in me may honor the oak tree, communicate with it, hug it, and nurture the soil around it. The Wiccan in me will do all this, and maybe ask for a branch so I can fashion a wand. As a Pagan I will plant, tend, and grow beautiful flowers and herbs for spiritual healing and good health. As a Wiccan I will do all this but maybe use some of the petals and herbs to create charms for specific purposes, such as attracting love or making incense for a Moon-honoring spell.

As a Pagan, I will value the wild creatures around me, seeing them as part of the whole of experience. Perhaps my Pagan path might lead me to explore the native cultures of animal guides and the legends of Diana as goddess of the hunt. I may even honor them in rituals. As a Wiccan I will try and seek out my special animal totem to receive knowledge. Perhaps I will look for a bear claw to make myself a talisman, and I will call upon Diana during a ritual to bring me protection when I go out camping in the woods.

As a Pagan I try to do my best to live with the natural cycles around me. As a Wiccan, I might try to alter them for mine or for the world's benefit, as the famous Witches of the Isle of Whyte did when they sold knotted ropes to charm the wind. I know this is where magic gets a bit sticky. As a Witch, I believe on drawing on the energy around me and using it, but you may wonder if you can honor nature and Mother Earth even while you are working it into your magic. Some Pagans don't believe you should mess with the natural cycles, that by reverence to the God and Goddess all will be taken care of the way it should.

Gaia, a solitary Pagan that I know, claims she can be a Pagan all on her own. "I can find the Way of the Goddess from readings and intuition. I can be a solitary practitioner. I am not always given a set of beliefs and knowledge. I do not cast spells, nor control the world around me for power. Wiccan people belong to groups, they have a long heritage of knowledge going back before we thought of writing down our thoughts. Most Wiccans are Pagans by definition."

Some Witches believe it is their right, their role to teach, to release, to bend and blend things, as long as the rules are followed. So who is right? And which way is better for you? Can you be a Pagan and a Wiccan too?

To be Pagan means to follow a path dedicated to nature and the cosmic life forces (of goddesses and gods) around us. According to the Pagan Federation, the three principles governing Pagans are :

1. Love for and kinship with nature. Reverence for the life force and its ever-renewing cycles of life and death.

2. The Pagan ethic: "If it harms none, do what thou wilt." This is a positive morality expressing the belief in individual responsibility for discovering one's own true nature and developing it fully, in harmony with the outer world and community.

3. Recognition of the divine, which transcends gender and acknowledges both the female and male aspect of deity. Communion with nature is something that is almost in a sense secondary. Self-explore first through meditation and conversing with the goddess. The need to commune with nature will come naturally through this.

According to Amanda, a friend who claims to be both Wiccan and Pagan, Wicca denotes outside rules and a collective organization. "A single person or selected few who act as the representative to the goddesses and lords. Paganism denotes inner rules. It is spiritualism collected from your own inner beliefs, from a series of different religions, from a moral code or conduct that you feel is right."

But Pagans themselves admit that there are many different types of Pagans. Like Wiccans they admire and support the choices of the individual in his or her quest to find the paths. Some will practice alone. Some will gather in groups especially around festival days. But all true Pagans will seek out and explore a deep connection with the natural world around them.

So if you plant a garden and say a prayer for growth, does that mean you're a Pagan? Probably. And if you fertilize it and whisper a spell to make it grow does that make you a Witch? Most likely, but I wouldn't go spreading it round the garden clubs in your neighborhood. Hey, even us heathens have got to keep some of our secrets!

Here, at long last, we see a difference forming between being a Pagan and being a Witch.

"I see Pagan as the more general term," says my friend Marilyn, who identifies herself more as a Pagan than a Wiccan, "those who don't worship a monotheistic religion. That could include Druidism. I see Wicca as specific to those who follow a more or less Gardenerian style or of the type Starhawk made famous. Anybody can do anything, with respect to spells and so on. This would be my take on it."

To quote Janet and Stewart Farrar: "Wicca is both a religion and a craft . . . As a religion—like any other religion—its purpose is to put the individual and the group in harmony with the divine creative principal of the cosmos, and its manifestation at all levels. As a craft, its purpose is to achieve practical ends by psychic means, for good, useful, and healing purposes."

But this doesn't mean diving into magic gives you free rein to go wild. Just because you *can* doesn't mean you *should*. Witches, too, have rules. Not only do they share the principle of "and ye harm none do what you will" with Pagans, they also have the threefold law: What you do comes back to you three times. So if you do good, you are sure to get rewarded. But if you do bad—by trying to take control over things you shouldn't or harming someone with your magic, it will come back and sting you, big time.

So bottom line here is forget the labels. I am proud to be "bi-religious"—both Pagan and Wiccan. And I explore these paths of mine with a profound sense of wonder. Like many who have walked before me, seeking the greatest of mysteries, I will find my own way through prayer, spell, or tradition, never forgetting to honor this natural world that has given me real magic and purpose in my life.

Pagan and Wiccan Elders

by Paniteowl

A long, long time ago—in the late 1960s—there was not a lot of information about alternative religions, but there were some authors whose works were beginning to show the promise of what was to come. Many of us devoured their words, and they melted into our lifestyles like cotton candy on the tongue. We were hungry for more, and in time the once sparse information became a feast—as the Neopagan community found voice.

In the glut of publications that have developed since then, we began to sift and nibble our way to understanding. We found truths, and we found lies. We found humor, and we found pathos. We found the glimmering shards of faith, and we found the bitter realities of charlatans and manipulators.

Yes, we were not so very different from any other cultural or religious group, for we were vulnerable in our search for answers to age-old questions. We persevered and found those teachers that spoke to our hearts and souls in a way that made sense, and we passed on what we learned, sharing our discoveries as we went along. The Neopagan community has grown on the foundation laid by those who shared their thoughts and their dreams through their books, poetry, artistry, and workshops.

The Passing of Elders

In recent years, as our community has grown and aged, we've seen the passing of elders such as Scott Cunningham, Doreen Valiente, Stewart Farrar, Lady Sheba, and Leo Martello, just to name a few. The loss of a bard or a storyteller is felt deeply by the Pagan heart. Still, in the aftermath of these losses a funny thing happened to some of us—we realized that people began to look at *us* as elders. How did that happen? I'm not old. I'm still studying and growing.

Still, whether I wanted it or not, the mantle of the elder was placed on my shoulders—and not too gently at times. Suddenly and inexplicably, I and many of my generation have become the crones and sages. What does this mean?

Looking at our community today, it amazes me to see the growth and the changes that have occurred in the last forty years, just as it shocks me to see the lines and wrinkles in the face that stares back at me from the mirror. The Pagan community is growing older, and there are many who have aged gracefully under its welcoming umbrella.

No, I'm not saying we're all doddering around in shawl and slippers, but there have been significant changes in the makeup

of our culture. Pagans now range across the full spectrum, from the newborn to the elder, and the Pagan culture is richer and stronger because of this.

Expanding through the Years

The Internet, of course, has had a great impact on the Pagan community. Everyone from youngsters, to middle-aged misfits, to a growing number of elders are on-line in chat rooms, websites, and e-mail lists. We seek information on attending festivals and gatherings, on the latest teachings, and the old stories as well as new tales of the recent history of Pagan culture. Where once we had to really search to find teachers, and others of like mind, we now have choices at our fingertips. We have seen the realization of the dreams of our ancestors.

Over the years I've met many people through my workshops—not just students, but other presenters, authors, and coven leaders. Too often we hear that people can't find teachers. The standard answer has always been, "The teacher will appear when the student is ready." Well, the community is ready for qualified teachers, and it really isn't difficult to find them at all. Itineraries and teacher biographies are posted on Internet sites. Many of the elders are contributing to journals and periodicals just like the one you're reading now.

A spiritual journey is not a "road trip." It is a life-long itinerary that takes us down many paths until we arrive at a certain destination. Some will start off with little more than a vague concept of what the world holds. Others draw maps, and plan diligently for the journey.

Looking at our community today, it amazes me to see the changes over the last forty years.

Some find themselves thrust upon the path without even realizing they are treading where others have gone before. Some break new trails, smoothing the path so that those who follow will have an easier time of it.

We often look to elders as guideposts on our tour, yet it is up to individuals to choose how that journey is accomplished. Sometimes, you can only catch glimpses of trailbreakers that have gone before you, but eventually all of us go a bit slower as we age. Instead of blazing new trails, we settle into a comfortable pace and enjoy the journey itself. We slow down so that others can catch up and listen to the stories of our journeys. We become the teachers. We become the elders. And we are surprised!

How I Found My Elder Self

Five years ago, a new festival was organized in New Jersey by the Mid-Atlantic Pagan Alliance. Held at Beltane, it is a wonderfully diverse and welcoming experience. I was proud when they asked me to be a presenter their first year, and I've made it a point to be available for them every year since.

Recently, it finally hit me that this is what being an elder is all about. In supporting this cause, I got a chance to see the growth of a community. I have seen children, who once were more interested in the playground than the workshops, now participating in classes. And they ask good questions. For them, a Pagan event is a natural part of their lives. They don't realize that just ten years ago, the events were few and far between. They assume that they have the right to practice their beliefs with others of their kind. They don't feel strange, or odd, or uneasy. What a wonderful thing to have happened.

Teenagers I met years ago are still coming to this event. Some have married, borne children, and now bring their families. Some have new jobs, and some have started their own businesses. They come to tell us of their accomplishments, and we are full of pride for them.

As I travel to different events throughout the year, I meet old friends and get a chance to compare notes about the community—how it is changing and growing, and so on. There are elders who give workshops and classes on everything from tarot readings, to croning and becoming the sage. They teach healing and the cultivation of herbs. They may stroll through your lives like a friendly neighbor, or roar through your consciousness like a wounded bear. The elders have their stories to tell, and sometimes they'd like to know you've paid attention.

As we dance around the bonfires with the young ones, we elders may not keep up the pace as well as we used to. We may sit out a few dances, and arthritis rub may be the "aromatherapy" scent you detect around us. We don't make walking sticks that merely look good, we actually use them to help get around as we pick our way through forest and glen, and up and down vendors row as we shop, talk, and network with our friends and neighbors in the community.

The Rising of Sirius

Last year it was my pleasure to join with three other crones to present workshops at the Sirius Rising event at Brushwood in Sherman, New York. We weren't sure what the response would be, but the four of us had worked together for some time in developing a series of talks—called "Cronespeak"—about the Pagan community itself.

The first workshop had a decent audience, and we were satisfied that there was an interest in what the crones had to say.

The second workshop doubled in size, as many people came back and brought others with them. Afterward, we found ourselves surrounded by young and old alike, asking questions and commenting on the material presented. They followed us back to our campsite, and conversation flowed through the night. The next morning, people were waiting at our doors to continue the talk.

It has become the custom at Sirius to hold a morning meeting. Hosted by Don Waterhawk, it's a chance to get to know one another and have a voice regarding the format of the festival. The crones participated each day, and more people came to know these elders as real people. By the time of our last workshop, there was room only to stand.

Truth be told, in the end we felt like we were teaching around the clock. There was no time during that week that our campsite was empty. We talked, we listened, we taught, and we learned, which is good. The crones and sages of our community can give advice on many topics, drawing from personal experience. Elders can give information on cultivating herbs, as well as practical advice on forming a coven. We can tell you what has worked in the past, and what has totally bombed, and why. We can talk about rites of passage, and give recipes for campfire meals. We can show you that magic works, and which gods and goddesses are alive and well in our community. We're not reading from books, we're talking from the heart and our experiences. We also know that people need to experience life for themselves, and all we can really do is serve as examples for those who come after us, just as we followed the examples set by our teachers and mentors.

A Few Elders in Our Community

When I think of elders in our community, a few come to mind immediately. Elspeth of Haven is always in great demand as she sets up her display of art done by Nybor. Her intensive workshop called "Resonating with the Crone" is a unique and uplifting experience. Don Waterhawk and Danielle are not old by any means, but their teachings and commitment to the community are ageless. Mike Short is a wonderfully colorful character, whose seasonal job is playing Santa Claus. He may really be Santa!

Dorothy Morrison, a "young" elder, shares her enthusiasm and love of life with everyone she meets. Janet Farrar, a wonderfully adept woman, shows how glamorous aging can be. Diane Des Rochers, author and political activist, shows how devastating a quick mind can be when dealing with officials. Rosemary Kooiman, of the Nomadic Chantry of the Gramery, offers a great example of strength and perseverance in the face of adversity. Elie Sheva is a wonderfully down-to-earth woman whose workshop "When Jews Were Pagan" gives new insight about the history of her heritage. Her teachings have touched me.

Betsy Ashbey and her partner Maggie provide many excellent opportunities for teachers and students to come together at their Blackwater Campground in Isle of Wight, Virginia. There, they host the spring and fall "Gathering of the Tribes" events. Cate and Frank Dalton, meanwhile, host "Craftwise" events in New York and Connecticut. They provide yet another opportunity for insight into the Pagan culture.

It would be impossible to list all of the elders in the community, but just know they are out there and more than willing to share stories and expertise. Most elders never stop seeking and celebrating life. They are an endless resource to draw from.

The Wisdom of Others

The community is maturing, changing, and adapting as we find our place in the greater community of humanity. There are many others in the Pagan community who have much to teach. They may not be old in years, but they are knowledgeable and dedicated to the community. You might call them "crones and sages in training." We elders learn from these people, at least as much as they learn from us. There are a great many Pagans who are old beyond their years. Life experience is unique for each of us. It doesn't take much effort to find those who have earned the respect of the community.

Becoming an elder is not a popularity contest. Many of us can be caustic, short tempered, crotchety, and downright ornery! Sometimes our patience is stretched thin to the breaking point. We are not all sweet little old ladies who bake cookies, nor the jolly old men who tell yarns on the porch, although we can be when we want to.

A few weeks ago, I took my ten-year-old granddaughter to visit relatives who are quite elderly. She had a great time wandering through the big old Victorian family home. She played with their dog, and we went out to dinner. We talked to her of our family history and told stories about those who have already passed on. We poured over photo albums, and we sifted through mementos of the past. We sang old songs, and played old tunes.

For me, it was a wonderful weekend, because we were giving her the gift of family. On the drive home, she was quiet. I asked her if anything was wrong, and she replied, "You're not like other grandmas."

I had to think quickly, and try to figure out what she meant by that. Was she disappointed in me? Was this an accusation or a compliment? So I asked her, and her reply tickled me. "Gram, you're different. You play drums, you go to festivals, you wear flowers in your hair, and you laugh a lot. You're always telling stories about how we should be. You sound like my teacher."

"It definitely feels like we haven't learned the lessons of intolerance and hatred."

I was surprised that this child was looking at me in a new light, and figuring out who I was as an individual, not just stereotyping me as an old woman. I may not always live up to her expectations of what a grandmother should be, but I will always be the best that I can be for her.

And so it is with the elders of the Pagan community. We may not always fit the image one has of an elder. To some, we may just be old people. To others, we may be respected as crones and sages. And to still others, we may be a frightening reminder of their own mortality. And that's just how it should be. We are the examples of the passage through life.

Crotchety Crone Musing

Don't tell me who I am. You don't know me!
Don't tell me who I should be. Show me!
Don't whine if others don't agree. Be strong!
Don't push! Invite, and I may go along.

I don't presume to know the path
That each of us must take.
I may mark out my trail for you,
But O, for Goddess sake!

The things that I enjoy and see
Are mine alone to weave.
It matters not what others think,
I know what I believe.

Jesus in the Circle:
Blending Christianity and Wicca

by S. Tifulcrum

It's relatively easy to imagine a Christian Witch, especially when you consider witch-craft as a set of techniques that can be employed by someone who practices any religion. It's not so easy to figure out how someone can blend Christianity and Wicca—two seemingly opposite religions with their own unique theologies.

I figured the best way to learn about anything is to go straight to the source, so that's exactly what I did—that is, I joined a few online e-lists dedicated to Christian Wicca. Over more than a year, I got to know some of these people, what they believed, how they practice, and the ultimate question: *why* they blend the two paths.

The diagram below shows where Christian Wicca fits into the spiritual intersection of traditions. The three major groupings are Christianity, Wicca, and the occult—which covers witchcraft and other esoteric systems and philosophies. The sizes of the overlapping areas are not to scale; this is just meant to show ideological overlap.

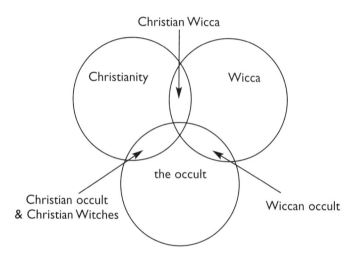

There are plenty of mystic or esoteric Christians who still don't use Wiccan practices in their personal path. Likewise, there are many Wiccans who dabble in Christian mythologies, but they don't make Christianity a dominant part of their Wiccan tradition. As I've always interpreted it, Wicca accepts the use of magic and witchcraft as part of the religion, so by default Wiccans are Witches. Some Wiccans do not self-identify as Witches, however, so the adage "some Wiccans are Witches but not all Witches are Wiccans" is appropriate.

I stress this right up front because a great deal of what is termed "Christian Wicca" is in reality esoteric or occult Christianity. Some of us use labels such as Christo-Pagan, Jesus Pagan, Goddess Christian, and so on, but this is not Christian

Wicca. Christian Wicca is the specific combining of two separate and distinct theological belief systems into a unique single spiritual path.

The group of practicing Christian Wiccans is relatively small, but it is rapidly growing—particularly with the explosion of chat forums and online bulletin boards where like-minded people can meet to discuss topics of interest. According to Autumn WolfSpirit, a Christian Wiccan who hails from Memphis, Tennessee, blending the two beliefs is really just an act of fulfillment. "I feel that I am truly where I need to be doing what I need to do."

Who are Christian Wiccans?

Just as Wicca and Christianity encompass people from all walks of life, so does Christian Wicca—former Catholic priests and monks, Wiccans with extensive training in diverse traditions, and spiritual seekers who were raised in other faiths. They are doctors, engineers, homemakers, teachers, students, artists, and so on. Christian Wicca has been around for many years but has become more well-known only in more recent times. At the same time, many strict Wiccans and Christians have treated this trend with negativity. Many believe the two religions should not be blended at all, so many Christian Wiccans feel it is safer to hide their spirituality.

Christian Wiccans tend to spend a lot of time discussing what to call themselves. It's probably this issue more than others that gets the most talk-time, although discussions about the use of magic and how exactly to combine the paths are also common.

What Do Christian Wiccans Believe?

Christian Wiccans tend to have a few things in common, no matter which religion is dominant in their spiritual path. First, they revere nature. Second, they acknowledge a feminine aspect of the divine—meaning Mary, the mother of Jesus, the Jewish concept of Sophia, or wisdom, or a feminine concept of the Holy Spirit.

Many incorporate a good deal of Jewish mysticism and practice into their faith, since Jesus was a Jew, after all.

Most Christian Wiccans will also note that there are some strikingly similar facets of Christianity and Wicca. Of particular interest is the connection between the Wiccan Rede– "Harm none, do as you will"–and the Christian Golden Rule–"Do to others as you would have them do to you." The format of the ritual of Christians and Wiccans–that is, the invocations, blessings, sharing of a ritual feast, and benedictions–is surprisingly similar.

Christian Wiccans who are primarily Wiccan in practice may simply use the Christian archetypes and pantheon within ritual much as they would any other pantheon–be it Greek, Roman, Egyptian, Norse, and so on. For these Christian Wiccans, it truly is a matter of having Jesus present in their circle.

> It's easy to imagine a Christian Witch, especially when you consider witchcraft as a set of techniques that can be employed by someone of any religion.

They may have chosen the Christian pantheon for many reasons: They were raised Christian and it is their heritage, or they want to be closer to the culture's mainstream religion. These people typically do not adhere to the philosophy that Christianity is the only true religion, and may call their path angel Wicca, trinitarian Wicca, Catholic craft, or something else.

Christian Wiccans who are predominantly Christian, however, face difficult challenges. Some do believe that Christianity is the only true religion, but they feel it lacks a feminine principle and so have chosen to make Wicca into something they can "fit" into their Christian practices. Other Christian Wiccans go to church and have circle rituals, and when confronted with the first of the Ten Commandments–"Thou shalt have no other gods before me"–they justify their practice by saying this means while God is supreme, other deities exist and can be worshipped if not elevated above him. Further, the Christian Wiccan trinity is often modified to include the female (Holy Spirit).

How Does Magic Fit in for the Christian Wiccan?

Magic is sometimes justified by Christian Wiccans by the argument that it was commonplace in the Biblical Old Testament. In fact, the use of magic was frequent enough that a book by Marvin Meyer and Richard Smith, *Ancient Christian Magic: Coptic Texts of Ritual Power*, compiles literally hundreds of spells, curses, rites, recipes, and amulets from the Egyptian Coptic Christians (ranging from the first to the twelfth century A.D.). It is unlikely that magic would have enjoyed such popularity anywhere if it was that sternly forbidden by the Bible.

Kitty F., from Chicago, Illinois, says her own view of magic is that it is the *duty* of every believer. "The original disciples of Jesus went out 'performing miracles'—what's the difference? Christians pray to a saint asking for help and call it 'divine intercession.' Christian Wiccans call to the divine and the angels to try to improve."

Autumn WolfSpirit agrees, saying: "I think that there is power in words, rituals, and deeds. I also believe that our faith fuels that power. I do use magic, because I believe that it is expected of me by my creator."

What about the Bible?

In many cases, Christian Wiccans have a near-encyclopedic command of the Bible, biblical history, and even some ancient Biblical languages. Christian Wiccans recognize that the Bible in its current form is not how the Bible originally appeared. It is well-known in academic circles that the Bible has at times included several other books that were later removed. Over time, the Bible was slowly standardized, essentially by the end of the fourth century. Because of thise uncertainly, however, most Christian Wiccans do not take the Bible literally, but they do view it as divinely inspired.

As for the infamous Bible verse, "Thou shalt not suffer a Witch to live" (Exodus 22:18), most Christian Wiccans know that this translation was an alteration made by King James in his own version of the Bible. King James was terribly afraid of Witches, as there were several attempts made by Witches to kill himself and his bride. King James also made a number of political changes to the Bible. Ambrose Hawk, a Biblical scholar and author of a book on scrying, says: "The original word [for Witch] in Hebrew does not directly translate [to modern English]. It seems to be a cross between our terms of 'sorcerer' and 'necromancer.' In the Greek,

235

this word was translated 'pharmacopeia'—a follower of Hecate who was believed to use the evil eye, curse others, and provide poisons . . . However, one should understand that this Witch is defined as somebody who has contracted with malign powers to gain the ability to magically harm others . . . ergo still not applicable to Wiccans." With that knowledge, most Christian Wiccans place no importance on that particular Bible verse.

The Bible is also but one of many texts that Christian Wiccans may draw from. They sometimes take into their practice books from mystic and Coptic Christians, the Dead Sea Scrolls, and other esoteric texts that have not been included in the current version of the Bible but that also describe the times in which Jesus lived and taught. Many of these texts reflect the cultures and mores of that time just as the Bible does. With a fuller depiction of the history and culture of Biblical times, Christian Wiccans feel more comfortable departing from the literal words printed in the Bible. In this way, they develop their own paths and relationships with Christian divinity and associated mythologies.

It's clear then how important a historical point of view is to the Christian Wiccan spiritual path. From this perspective, emphasis is placed more on morals and values rather than dogma and prescribed ritual.

Reconciling Christianity and Wicca

How on earth can a Christian Wiccan combine the two different religious theologies and not develop a split personality? The answer to this question varies according to each person, but in the end it comes down to how Christian Wicca is approached.

Christianity generally claims that it is the only true religion, and all others are false. However, many Christian Wiccans point to genealogical evidence in the Bible, particularly dealing with the growth of Adam's lineage, that indicates other people with other religions existed at the time. In addition, there is a certain amount of skepticism as to how much of the "one and only" message is really "churchianity"—that is, church teaching.

Many Christian Wiccans consider themselves to be extremely good Christians. They have developed personal relationships with Jesus and other Christian deities, and in many cases actually do tend to practice what is preached better than the average Christian. The fact that some worship in a circle rather than a church is of little or no consequence to them, and they cite Matthew 18:20—"For where two or three are gathered in my name, I am there among them."

On the other hand, many Christian Wiccans are also active members in an organized church—albeit typically a liberal one such as a Universalist Unitarian or nondenominational church. Episcopal and Methodist churches are also often more accepting of liberal Christian views, as are churches with a high concentration of college student members. Of course, attitudes can and do vary from congregation to congregation, so Christian Wiccans may visit a number of churches before finding one that suits. Once they do though, it is often a love of ritual and community that sustains these church memberships, or the sense of continuation from childhood church attendance.

Why Blend at All?

Since many do attend Christian churches, the question begs to be asked: Why blend the two paths at all?

Aroha, a three-year Christian Wiccan from Wellington, New Zealand, says she was led in spirit to blend the paths. "I felt that this is truly the way for me to best express my religious beliefs, and *live* them. I am Christian, who has found Wicca to be my way to express and live my beliefs."

According to Kitty F., Christianity and Wicca do not meet her spiritual needs individually because Christianity misses out on the feminine aspect of the Divine. "The 'Holy Spirit' is mentioned in passing. Although She grants many miracles to the disciples of Christ, She is all but ignored as an individual aspect of Divine. Wicca does not recognize Jesus the Christ. I truly believe He came to us as Man and sacrificed Himself for us."

After all this research and interaction with Christian Wiccans, I've come to some very definite conclusions. Chrysalis, a five-year Christian Wiccan from Fort Wayne, Indiana, is a Christian Wiccan by marital circumstance rather than by choice. I tend to agree with her when she says: "It is very possible to combine Christianity with Wicca, meaning making a tradition of Wicca, but it is next to impossible to combine Wicca with Christianity, meaning making it a denomination of Christianity."

It does seem to be much easier to make Christianity a tradition of the more flexible Wiccan path, than it is to work from the other direction. But to those who live each day blending the two religions, I have nothing but the utmost respect for their determination to live a life of spiritual journey and relationship with the divine—no matter what face the divine may wear.

The Sacred Rites of Initiation

by Flame RavenHawk

If you are a practicing solitary Witch, are you missing out by not having a coven initiation? Are you really a "Wiccan" without seeking this ritual?

These are just two of the are many questions asked in the Wiccan community regarding the form, function, and requirements of the formal Wiccan initiation. The debate is complicated by a lack of agreement about what an initiation really is, and why it's important. Everyone brings their own definitions and expectations to the subject, leading to misunderstandings.

239

According to established traditions, most notably Gardnerian, initiation is a prerequisite to the full acceptance and participation into the coven and tradition. Some even go so far as to say that one cannot be a Wiccan without such an initiation. Formal traditions focus on the rite of initiation as an entry to the "mysteries," and they get very mysterious when talking about it to noninitiates.

However, through the encouragement of many traditionally initiated Wiccans such as Scott Cunningham and Raymond Buckland, Wicca has blossomed more recently into a flexible and evolving tradition. They teach a form of Wicca that doesn't depend on initiation or lineage, and instead encourages the practice of "self-dedication." This new tradition is more accessible to the solitary seeker. There are now many dedicated elders within the Wiccan community who continue to practice and teach Wicca without ever having the benefit of the formal initiation. They justifiably feel that their work is valid despite this lack.

So what is initiation good for exactly, and why is it the subject of such heated debate and controversy?

Initiation vs. Dedication

First, let's clarify what we're talking about—a lot of the debate and confusion stems from a basic misunderstanding of terms. A spiritual initiation, as we are using the word, is actually a very specific term with a limited and precise definition. Many people mistakenly confuse the term "initiation" with the term "dedication," and use them interchangeably. According to *Webster's Unabridged Dictionary*, to *initiate* means "1. to bring into practice or use; to introduce by first doing or using; 2. to teach the fundamentals of some subject to; to help (someone) to begin doing something; 3. to admit as a member into a fraternity, club, etc., especially through use of sacred ceremony or rights."

The first definition infers a new beginning. When we initiate actions, we are beginning something new. Although this first

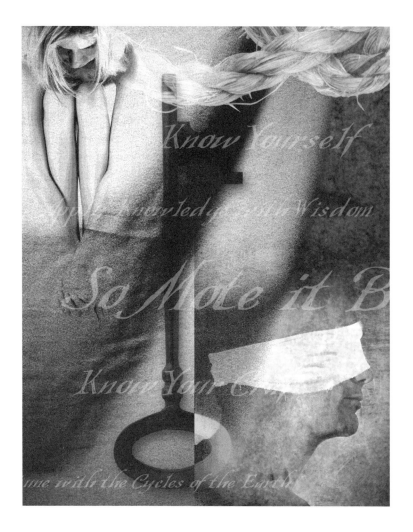

use of the word doesn't directly relate to spirituality, it is still implied in our spiritual use of the term. When we undergo initiation, we begin a new spiritual life.

Definitions two and three describe the spiritual use of initiation. Initiation is the process of teaching the fundamentals needed to begin a practice. It is also the ceremony that admits the new Wiccan into the specific lineage or tradition. As defined above, we can see that an initiation cannot typically be performed by oneself. An initiation requires the special skills of one who has been previously initiated. We can teach ourselves information from books, but the knowledge received through initiation is, by definition, provided by others.

So what are we supposed to learn via initiation that we can't get from books? Initiation ideally leads us to a new spiritual understanding. Its purpose is not to acquire simple factual knowledge, instead initiation leads us to the direct experience of the divine. It requires another person because, generally speaking, we can't lead ourselves to a place we've never been before. By this definition, a "self-initiation" is simply an experience that happens to us, not something we are able to create on our own.

Complementing the rite of initiation is the dedication ceremony. According to Webster, "dedicate" means "to set apart and consecrate to a deity or to a sacred purpose; to devote to a sacred use, by a solid act or by religious ceremonies." Many solitary Wiccans have chosen to honor their devotion to their gods and goddesses and the path of Wicca by creating a dedication ritual. Contrary to initiation, a dedication does not require anyone but the person seeking to affirm their commitment to their path. A dedication is a formal expression of commitment. Dedication ceremonies can be a beautiful and powerful way of expressing a personal, intimate relationship to deity. In a dedication ceremony, the dedicant proclaims his or her identity as a Witch before the gods, and he or she claims a heritage of spiritual independence. The dedicant reaches out and offers his or her life to a spiritual path or a specific deity. Typically, this ritual is a profound and personally moving one.

In discussions, however, many Pagans mistakenly consider initiation and dedication synonymous. They're not. As we've seen, although they might appear to be similar an initiation specifically requires knowledge, guidance, and direction.

So now we know what initiation is, you may ask why it is considered so important to the tradition? To understand the answer, we must move beyond the petty idea that formal initiation is merely the right of recognition that lets a person into some secret club. On one level, initiation does play the role of confirming one's status within

> **Everyone brings their own definitions and expectations to the subject of initiation, leading to many misunderstandings.**

a recognized tradition. While this idea of initiation certainly plays a valuable role within more formalized groups, this is in reality the lesser role of initiation. For those practicing within an initiatory tradition, the rite of initiation is far more profound and invested with a much deeper purpose. It is the ultimate journey into the unknown—a journey that is led by the initiators.

The Role of Initiation

Since the resurgence of Pagan spiritual thought began in the late '50s, the subject of initiation has been hotly debated. As originally presented and taught by Gerald Gardener and the early founders of the practice, Wicca is defined as a "mystery tradition." Like the ancient Eleusinian mysteries in Greece, Wicca contains secret religious rites and knowledge that are kept apart from the mundane public realm. It's not secret due to some perverse desire to be a spiritual "elitist," but due to the very real recognition that some things simply cannot be coherently discussed without the context of this shared experience. And like Eleusis, these secrets can only be revealed, not merely told.

In Eleusis, participants were led through secret rites wherein the mysteries of Demeter and Persephone were revealed and the very secrets of life and death itself were dramatically demonstrated. Rather than simply telling the story of the goddesses in a less-than-structured setting, the process of gradually unfolding and revealing knowledge helped to guide the participant to greater insights. The simple mythological facets of the story do not greatly move us. However, the pageantry and structure of the ceremonies and rites produce a deep change in the hearts of the participants, awakening a deeper awareness that transforms everyone involved.

Although the exact details have been lost through the mists of time, what has been told by witnesses to those rites is revealing. Initiation into the Eleusinian mysteries was a voyage into the unknown, with life-transforming knowledge to be found on the other side. As far as we can tell from recorded accounts of initiates, the experience was deep and profoundly moving. That the rites continued for hundreds of years attest to the potency and value for those involved. And the vehicle for this personal transformation was the rite of initiation. The "secret" wisdom contained in the Eleusinian mysteries was passed on from an initiate of the mysteries to the seekers, thus preserving both the secrecy and the sacredness of the wisdom that was imparted.

The Sacred Rite

The very term "sacred" has built into its definition the idea of being set apart from the mundane world. The root of the word, as well as the word "consecrate," is the Latin word *sacre,* which means "to set apart, or to make holy." Reserving knowledge to set it apart and make it holy is an ancient and time-honored practice. Since our earliest recorded history—from the time of towering pyramids to that of drive-through funerals—we see cultures honor those things they consider sacred by setting them apart from mundane life.

Traditional Wicca has followed this ancient formula. Although much of the detailed information within Wicca is now public knowledge and freely available to any with the desire to seek it and the wit to understand it, many of the elements that make Wicca a "mystery tradition" remain. There are still some things that are preserved as sacred and secret among some traditions, such as the names of certain gods and goddesses. There are

244

hidden meanings to some tools, and of course the actual initiation rituals themselves are kept hidden. Ultimately though, it's not secret information that makes initiation so sacred. Initiation is sacred because it marks the initiate, setting them apart from the mundane world.

Like the Eleusinian mysteries, understanding the mythological story of Demeter and Persephone does not have the same impact as directly experiencing the goddesses. Similarly, traditional Wiccans do not feel that the true heart of the tradition can be found in a book. The initiation ceremony is considered essential to opening up the pathways to the divine. The study prepares the initiate, but the actual initiation is the final act of opening the door. Initiated Wiccans feel that there is a core experience that lies at the heart of Wicca. It is this core experience that is sought in the rite of initiation.

The Initiation Experience

Ideally, an initiation is a rite of passage that carries the initiate from a state of ignorance to a state of knowledge. Keep in mind, however, the knowledge imparted during initiation are not just the secrets of a coven. An initiation is designed to guide the initiate along the ultimate journey into the unknown, and the ultimate destination is the divine presence.

An initiation experience is a profound and deeply felt spiritual experience. Initiation lifts a person out of normal perceptions, and brings the person to a place where he or she can confront the gods. It is transcendent. Ideally, whether performed within a traditional group or performed on one's own behalf, an initiation opens up the psychic channels that connect the initiate to a direct experience of deity. An initiation should be a transformative experience, and one that will have an impact on the rest of one's life.

Initiation is an important experience in spirituality. It can and does transform lives. However, self-transformation is difficult in a vacuum. We exist in relation to the world around us. As such, this experience is easier to accomplish when guided by someone who has had a similar experience. We need someone who is familiar with this experience to lead us to that place ourselves. How can we reveal a mystery to ourselves, if we don't know what the mystery is?

This is the basis for the case in favor of coven initiations. The ritual is specifically designed to lead the seeker down an unknown path that is only familiar to one already initiated. We're not talking about the secret "mechanics" of the ritual, but the mystery of the destination. The ritual should lead the seeker to the threshold of the divine, and the initiation experience leads the person through that door.

A noninitiate might know that such a door exists, but not know how to find it. The theory is that you can only be guided to that place by one who knows where it is—someone who has already "been through the door."

Still, isn't it possible that one can have an amazing, transcendent experience without the benefit of an initiation ritual? Of course. If a solitary Wiccan does not have a guide to lead him or her through this experience, the gods themselves have been known to step in. Remember that, by definition, initiation requires knowledge from outside of ourselves. God and goddess are the ultimate, original initiators. The question then becomes how can solitary practitioners encourage, create, or inspire this unknown experience for themselves?

The Challenge

How do you inspire yourself to have a spiritual epiphany? Most people stumble across moments of awe-inspiring connection through regular practice of spiritual techniques such as meditation, magic, and prayer. Sometimes a private moment or personal ritual becomes so profound that the gods reach through of their own accord. And history is full of accounts of people who receive this experience spontaneously, with little or no advance preparation.

The proof of the experience is the change that it inspires. For many, the most immediate difference is noticed in relationship to deity. Instead of the existence of deity being a matter of faith, it becomes a matter of personal certainty. You no longer simply "believe" in a god and goddess, you know them. They are as real and immediate as the ground beneath our feet.

The experience opens the awareness to a reality that is richer and more complex than previously conceived, and yet the veil is pulled aside to reveal the simple beauty of it all. A deeper sense of connection to both the world of spirit and the world of form is typical, and results in a change in outlook. For example, the initiate often reports feelings of extra self-assurance. After getting a peek into the cosmic consciousness, the initiate feels more secure in the knowledge that there is an underlying pattern to life.

Many initiates also report growing more intuitive after this experience. Although they have typically been learning about the intuitive arts as part of their preparation for initiation, they often find that psychic gifts are strengthened and more reliable than they were before. Some report that they gain new spiritual knowledge directly from deity. A feeling of being directly inspired by a divine presence is typical.

And finally, the initiate gains the serenity that comes with finding a deeper purpose in life. Life itself, in all of its richness and complexity, is an amazing mechanism of spiritual expression. The epiphany that is produced in the sacred rite of initiation allows us to see our place in the grander scheme of the universe. It is both humbling and inspirational, and we come away transformed.

Judy Harrow, a respected Wiccan high priestess and founder of the Proteus Coven (a Gardnerian-derived tradition) summarizes it perfectly when she says: "Other initiations are carefully structured rituals, something that our elders do to and for us. Witchcraft is one such initiatory Path. Initiations and elevations are our greatest acts of magic. They work by separating us from ordinary contexts and mindsets, disorienting us, carrying us to the liminal state, the threshold of change. A candidate for initiation must let go completely, trust himself utterly to the elder or initiator."

Whether the initiator is a fellow confidant in the craft, or is a god or goddess, above all else a dedicant is asked to open his or her spirit to the possibility of change during initiation—the kind of change that leads to a new life. By seeking the experience of connection, we grow beyond the limits of our normal way of viewing the world. We see the beauty and sanctity of the earth expressed in our own hearts. The doorway to the sacred lies within, if only we ask to find it.

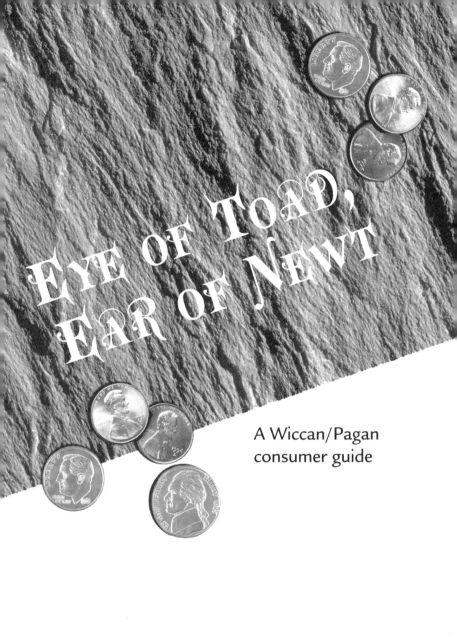

Eye of Toad, Ear of Newt

A Wiccan/Pagan
consumer guide

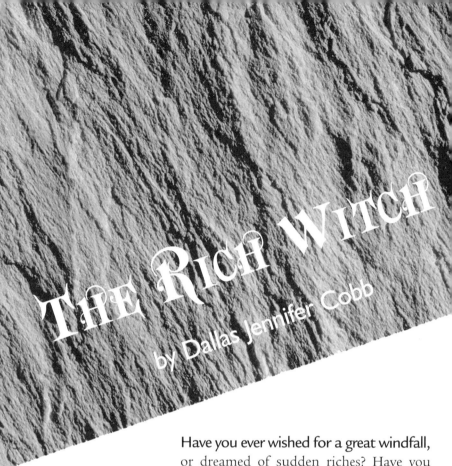

THE RICH WITCH

by Dallas Jennifer Cobb

Have you ever wished for a great windfall, or dreamed of sudden riches? Have you mused over get-rich-quick schemes, or wondered if there's such a thing as a sure bet? If so, then this article is probably not for you.

This is an article about abundance, but not about the abundance of money or material possessions. Rather, these are my thoughts about seeking, and finding wealth in all realms of life.

Imagine tapping into your deepest dreams for riches, and feeling empowered to plant the seeds of prosperity through

250

becoming a Rich Witch

"My wealth is growing."

lots of friends loving relationships nice home fulfil ca

secret compartment purse

Define prosperity.

Give thanks by tithing and gift-giving.

Practice money spells and rituals.

rituals and practices. And imagine through this, you can culti-vate real wealth throughout your life.

It can be done.

I am living proof. Truth be told, I am a fabulously wealthy person. I am rich with time, energy, health, wisdom, love . . . and money. And I can tell you my secrets for becoming a rich Witch. It is easier than you think.

First, say with me, five times quickly: "Rich Witch. Rich Witch. Rich Witch. Rich Witch. Rich Witch."

There. Now you're focused, attentive and present in the moment. These are the skills needed to cultivate abundance and prosperity. Above all else, becoming a rich Witch demands these things: focus, attention, and presence.

The Fundamentals of Luck

Chance and luck are statistically predictable occurrences. An actuary or mathematician will tell you that odds are fixed and predictable. While they can't predict who will enjoy winning, or precisely when luck will happen, they can with great accuracy tell us precisely how many people in one hundred will experience a certain kind of luck.

Lotteries are founded on this knowledge, as are most sorts of contests. The bad news is that the odds are usually, purposefully, low. And it is not possible to alter the odds without "fixing" or "rigging" a contest, lottery, or game. But, there is good news.

We can influence chance and luck. Focus and attention create intention, improving the odds of winning by creating a space for luck to land. Everything in the universe is composed of energy that can attract, repel, or charge an item, person, or circumstance. By altering consciousness, a person can alter an energy state, and thereby "charge" the self with intention.

Good luck is a state of mind. I am rich, indeed. I am lucky. At times I feel a sense of all possibility being open to me, of good things coming my way, a sense of the bounty of life. I feel lofty and secure, comfortable. I believe that it is this expansive feeling that opens me up to the awareness of goodness in my life. The more aware I am of fortune, the more good fortune I experience.

When we are present, attentive, and focused, our intention to feel the wealth of the world opens us to receiving wealth. Enjoyment of the small blessings of the day and an awareness of the good that abounds can actually make us rich with goodness. The more you choose to love, the more loving you will feel, and the more love you will receive.

Luck has to occur somewhere, so choose to let it begin with you. Realize that you can influence luck and chance through focus and attention. The act of being present, optimistic, and aware of opportunities is what manifests luck. These are the practices of the rich Witch.

Rich Witch Rules

Several universal truths and rules govern prosperity magic.

First, the manifestation of abundance and wealth is an ongoing practice. There is no sudden, one-time change, but a process through which abundance is cumulatively attracted.

Second, you are responsible for creating space in your life for good things. If you consciously choose to let go of things that no longer suit you, you can open up space and energy for what you desire. When you give stuff away, it can be done consciously, with gratitude and thankfulness. Getting rid of physical clutter can help rid you of emotional and mental clutter.

Generosity is a circular energy. The practice of letting go is a fundamental part of prosperity magic. When we give gifts or make donations, we contribute to the continuation of the circular energy of generosity. We don't give so that we can receive, but in the practice of giving we create the energy of generosity. It flows away, around, and eventually back to us. Which leads to the next rule.

What goes around, comes around. You attract what you express. Good deeds beget good deeds, and positive thoughts produce positive results. Using our own tools of focus—prayer, meditation, trance, and intention—attracts good energy to us and influences the odds.

Mother Theresa and St. Francis of Assisi had the idea right. Instead of expecting to be loved, you should love someone. Don't seek to be understood, but try instead to understand. When you hunger for something, try feeding someone else. Fill the world with good.

Sometimes what goes around can really come back to you in a big way. Many practicing Pagans will remind you of the laws of threefold: Be careful what you wish for, it can come back to you threefold. Consider this when casting spells or doing magical

...you are responsible for creating space in your life for good things.

Ganesha — God of good luck. Invoke a God or Goddess.

Practice under the Magical Moons

Reduce, Reuse, Recycle

work that involves other people. On the other hand, ask and you shall receive. Through the ages this adage has expressed what we all know. If you can but ask for help, your call will be answered. All good is given if you ask for it.

It is important to be clear, to know yourself, your wants, and your needs, and to clearly state what they are. Be specific. If you are trying to manifest a new home through prosperity magic, don't say, "Oh, anything will do," when asked what you are looking for. Sometimes just telling friends the whimsical version of what you desire can manifest it instantly, because they may have, or know of someone who has, exactly what you are seeking.

As above, so below. This is the deep truth. If you don't believe that you are worthy, how will you manifest wealth in your life? If your life is in shambles, start the very personal work of tidying house. Do the work needed to feel that you are deserving of good. When your house is in order, your life will be a testament to your worth. When you feel worthy, good things will befall you. When you radiate goodness, good things happen.

Make the time to practice rich Witch magic regularly. Set up symbols on your altar and in your home that will help you to pause momentarily and affirm your worth. Commit yourself.

Riches in Every Realm

Manifestation of wealth happens the physical, mental, emotional, social, and spiritual spheres. Attention to each of these can help focus and clear your intentions. Take a look at how you live. Are you a person who is perceived as a valuable contributing member of the community? Or are you careless and needy?

While some Pagans believe you shouldn't use magical intention to attain material goods, others believe it is permissible. My suggestion is if you are going to try to conjure wealth, do it in an ethical manner. Include phrases like "for the good of all involved" and "according to free will."

Manifesting physical wealth should always be followed with thanksgiving and an active sharing of the wealth. There is nothing liberating or empowering about living in poverty, so stretch your imagination and conjure up some physical wealth to help yourself and others.

Also, take time to think about how wealth and prosperity can influence what you manifest. Your mental state can either enrich or impoverish your circumstances. Do you think the cauldron is half empty or half full? How do you define prosperity? Given a positive perspective, many of us find that we are far wealthier than we ever thought.

When we constantly worry that we are not good enough, not worthy, or there is not enough to go around, then we are resonating with negative energyy. Too often, we get separated from our sense of self, and forget that we are part of the abundant universe. We somehow stop believing in it, and focus instead on a perceived lack. In this state of mind it is difficult to recognize the good fortune we have.

Being comfortable with yourself, your Pagan identity, and your magical power can transform your life. Confidence and security radiate from you and draw prosperity. Emotional wealth can include feeling loved, happy, and free. When you believe in yourself, and that you are deserving, you eliminate the restrictive beliefs that keep you from manifesting abundance. Lack of self-confidence will limit the effect of your magic and what you can manifest. Social wealth is a sphere that is often overlooked. An abundance of friends and secure, loving relationships makes for a fabulously rich Witch. Get connected with your family and active in your community. Make daily conversations rich with good intention. Infuse your community with light and love, and it will radiate back to you.

Attention to spiritual wealth lets us feel good about our spiritual path. For each of us, our spiritual practices will differ. Whether in a coven, a circle, or a solitary practitioner, you need to connect to your own reasons for being a Pagan. Feeing good about spiritual choices will promote a sense of well-being.

Giving Thanks

Sometimes I think all I really need to do is to give thanks, but thanksgiving serves several important purposes: Acknowledging the benevolence of the universe and the abundance it provides keeps the energy of generosity alive, and circulates synchronicity and luck. Tangible methods of giving thanks include tithing, gift giving, and cultivating awareness of good deeds and actions.

Tithing

Traditionally, tithing is intended for you to give back to the source of your spiritual nourishment. It has been used by churches and is currently used by nonprofit organizations, charities, and social groups. As a rule, community members are asked to pledge 5 percent of their earnings to the organization. This perpetuates a circular energy of generosity and teaches us to let go and not worry about lack. The act of giving away cultivates a feeling of magnanimous prosperity and expansive wealth.

When you tithe, be thankful. Choose the organization, group, or cause that you want to support, and give generously to them without expectation of return or recognition.

Gift Giving

Giving gifts is a tangible way of saying thank you to an individual. Try to give thanks for each and every good act that someone does, acknowledging how it enriches your life. Whether it is a special occasion, a visit to someone's house, or a happy day, take a gift along. Gift giving is also an investment in a relationship. It is by giving that we become truly wealthy. When you have innumerable friends and relatives that you can count on, then you are rich. Relationships, like bank accounts, require regular deposits in order to facilitate withdrawals.

Riches and Rituals

Money Spells

Linda, my daughter's fairy godmother, sticks a penny in Terra's pocket and whispers: "May you always have money." My grand-

Make time to practice Rich Witch magic regularly.

mother made purses and bags out of every imaginable material. She always put money in a small secret pocket, so the purse would never be empty.

Want to work some rich Witch money magic every day? Place a small urn or bowl near where you place your keys or empty your pockets. Each night empty your loose change into the urn, and say, "My wealth is growing." When the Moon is full, empty the urn and to the accumulated abundance exclaim: "I am rich indeed."

While you wash dishes, run the tub, or water the garden, affirm: "Like water flowing, my riches are growing." Use this affirmation, or scribe your own: "All is well in my world. The Goddess loves me and will provide for me. My trust makes everything possible. I put my faith in the bounty of the universe."

Plant a money plant in your garden, consciously creating space for more wealth in your life and vowing to grow abundant.

As the plant grows, be aware of the growing energy of wealth surrounding you. In the fall, harvest the silver dollar–shaped blooms, and take them indoors. Place some on your altar, and say: "Riches have an honored place in my life."

When you are out and about, keep your awareness of riches open. Remember the old saying: "Find a penny, pick it up, all day long you'll have good luck. If a friend you chance to see, give it to them for luck times three."

When you find treasures, money, or other riches, always give thanks. I often say: "Thank you, Goddess, for your generosity. I welcome your abundance in every form."

Respect riches, and value wealth. Never throw away money, not even pennies. Using coins for magic work, or wishes, is not throwing them away, it is investing in magic. Giving coins to panhandlers or musicians is investing in the circular energy of generosity. If you see money on the ground, pick it up, give thanks for the found wealth, and know you are valuing riches.

Smudging for Clarity

Smudging removes stagnant vibrations from our energy bodies, and environment, and can invoke a sense of well-being. To promote a positive mental state, try smudging to clear your aura. Use sweet grass, sage, cedar, and other herbs that resonate with you—lavender for calm, mugwort for protection, clary sage for wisdom.

Drawing Magic

Drawing magic is used to draw people, things, energies and situations to you. It can be performed at the altar, table, or desk, or can be visualized almost anywhere. You will need a piece of string about three feet long, a small square of paper, and a pen.

Sitting at the table, meditate on what it is you seek to draw to you. Be specific. Write it on the piece of paper, adding, "its equivalent or better." If you are trying to draw a person or living being to you be sure to add: "according to free will." As you fold the paper, focus on the situation and let your desires flow. As you fold the paper, know you will soon hold your desires.

Now, tie the string around the paper. Holding one end of the string, throw the paper over the far edge of the table, out of sight. As you pull the string, and subsequently the paper, toward you, focus on what you want to draw to you. Picture it happening, making space for it. Stay fully focused until finally you have drawn the paper into your hands. Now feel the reality of what you have wished for.

Keep the packet with you, tucked in your pocket or safely placed on your altar. Continue to give attention and focus to the wish, and practice drawing magic. You may be amazed by how powerful this spell can be. The use of simple tools to activate our focus and intention can attract much of what we desire.

Rich Witch Goddesses and Gods

The Pagan tradition is full of gods and goddesses who are associated with the practice of rich Witch magic. Learn their stories, and familiarize yourself with the energies of prosperity and abundance. And, when you are doing magic, invoke a god or goddess to help you. Below are some deities you can call on.

Anu, the Celtic (Irish) goddess of plenty. Invoke her help with manifestation magic, fertility, and prosperity.

Apa, the Indian goddess of waters, cleansing, and purification. She symbolizes life, immortality, health, wealth, prosperity, and longevity.

Fauna, the Latin goddess of the earth, wildlife, forests, and fertility. She symbolizes prosperity.

Frey, the Norse God of sunshine and rain. He brings the bountiful harvest and symbolizes peace and prosperity.

Ganesh, the Hindu elephant-headed god of wisdom. She symbolizes good fortune and prosperity.

Lakshmi, the Indian goddess of good fortune and prosperity. She represents all that is feminine, and is beauty personified.

Lu-Hsing, the Chinese god of salaries, wages, and employment. He and symbolizes success, prosperity, and earned wealth.

Magical Moons

In July the Mead Moon, also known as the Blessing Moon, brings a time of health, success, rebirth, and strength. It's time of the first harvests, perfect to gather your magical herbs.

August's Barley Moon is a time of plenty. It is a time to celebrate the abundance of your garden, to make an offering to the Goddess, give thanks for Gaia's fertile goodness, and to plan ahead for the coming months. The Barley Moon is also a good time to look for promotion within the workplace.

In September, the Harvest Moon brings a time for protection of our wealth, guarding of our crops, and harvests. This is the time to celebrate abundance and prosperity.

The Hunter's Moon in October brings a time for reflecting on the previous year's accomplishments, setting new goals, and clarifying intentions. It is also a good time for divination and looking into the future.

During November, the Snow Moon is also a good time to use divination to find out what is in store for the near future and to work with prosperity and the bonds of family and friends.

Live Long and Prosper

While it is important we remember our relationship to the Earth, and not engage in conspicuous consumption or throw away consumerism, it is time for Pagans to embrace abundance.

While many in our communities still distrust a materialistic society, we need to acknowledge that living abundantly, as rich Witches, doesn't necessarily result in excessive consumption. We can start by investing in this simple belief: We are worthy. And knowing this will lead to purely good things.

Let your dreams rise, and pursue them. Make the practice of abundance a regular part of your life, and see what riches come.

Shopping for Herbs Online

by Chandra Beal

Carlos Casteneda once defined herbs as the plants of wisdom. And in fact, herbs have long been used for their healing and magical energies. A selection of herbs is indispensable to any magical practitioner. They are versatile and can be ground into powders, placed in gris-gris bags, rubbed into candles for spells, and used in ointments and other medicinal potions. Herbs purify the air and dispel negative energy in sacred spaces. Whether used fresh or dried, brewed in tea or burned in offering, herbs are an essential element in every magical home.

The advent of the Internet has made shopping for magic tools and accessories a breeze. No longer does one have to drive to the nearest metropolis to stock up on mugwort and dowsing rods. Now you can just point and click.

Still, shopping online can also be overwhelming because of the sheer volume of items to choose from. The quality of merchandise and level of customer service can vary greatly. Buying herbs online can be especially problematic because of their perishable nature. You can't touch or smell the herbs to see how fresh they are. This guide is intended to help you shop smartly for herbs online, narrow your choices, and select the best herbs and suppliers for your needs.

E-Shopping for Herbs Tips

If you are new to shopping online, there are a few things you should know before you dive in. Since you can't judge the character of a shop by face-to-face contact, you need to become an informed shopper. Before you hit that "send" button, be sure you understand the company's policies and what exactly you are purchasing, what fees apply, and what your rights are as a consumer.

Prices and services vary greatly, so shop around and compare. Most online shops accept credit cards and electronic payments such as PayPal. Many still accept personal checks and money orders. A few even offer layaway plans for large purchases.

Remember always to figure shipping costs into your order. You may be able to save a bit on shipping and get your goods faster if you order from a company in your area. Be especially careful when buying heavy items such as salt or cauldrons. It may be cheaper to buy such things locally and avoid the shipping costs based on weight. Delivery methods and return policies vary greatly. Familiarize yourself with these before making your final purchase. Be sure to print a copy of your order for your records.

Also pay attention to the actual size or amount of items, whether herbs are powdered or cut, or other such details so you don't get surprised.

Privacy today is becoming increasingly important to consumers, especially online. Pagans in particular are sensitive to this issue because of the misconceptions long surrounding their beliefs. Most shops worth their salt display their privacy policies on their web site. It should disclose what information is being collected on the site in

question and how that information is being used. If you don't see anything posted regarding privacy, ask the proprietor for more information. Find out how orders are packaged and labeled, and ask if orders over the website are electronically encrypted to protect your personal information. See if they have a physical or mailing address, and phone and fax number so you have some recourse if their website suddenly disappears. If a site owner is unwilling to disclose this type of information, move on. You can also check with the local Better Business Bureau if you have questions about a company's reputation.

When you're shopping online, you can't smell the herbs or judge their quality by sight or texture. Ask the proprietor how long products sit on the shelf or how fresh they are. Some companies may let you try a sample first. Others offer a paper catalog via snail mail that may give you a better idea of the quality of items, and ensure that the company is legitimate.

Many Pagan commerce sites also have chat rooms or online community links so you can find fellowship among others with similar interests. Several have free electronic newsletters focusing on different topics, or free articles and recipes. The Internet is a wealth of information and a great source for an almost endless array of herbs and herbal supplies.

Some Recommended Herbal Websites

Pagan Herbal Shops

Magickware
www.magickware.com
7657 Winnetka Ave. #102
Canoga Park, CA 91306

Magickware specializes in Wiccan and Pagan supplies and occult and metaphysical information and products. Their herbal products include essential oils, incense, dried herbs, resins, powders, and roots. They also offer several blended herbs for specific purposes and accessories such as smudge sticks, charcoal, and decorative containers. The most helpful aspect of their site is an A-to-Z table of magical herbal correspondences for creating spell kits. Magickware also carries mojo bags, bath salts, altar supplies, gemstones, jewelry, crystal balls, and metaphysical books.

Ladyhawk's Treasures
www.ladyhawkstreasures.com
320 Stonecastle Avenue
Reisterstown, Maryland 21136
(800) 393-0368

If you are primarily interested in herbs with magical correspondences, Ladyhawk has a nice selection of herbs such as mandrake, mugwort, and damiana. They are available whole and powdered. They also carry mortar and pestle sets, glass jars for storage, and a few herbal tea blends. Ladyhawk has a good selection of incense burners, cauldrons, jewelry, clothing, books, music, and altar supplies.

New Moon Occult Shop
www.newmoonoccultshop.com
P.O. Box 110
Didcot, Oxon OX11 9YT
United Kingdom
44 (0)1235 819744

Many Celtic recipes call for herbs native to the United Kingdom that can be hard to find. Based in England, New Moon has an large selection of dried herbs—from Agnus Castus (chaste tree) to yellow dock. Alongside the traditional herbs you'll find herbal cigarettes, resins, and Bach flower remedies. Keep in mind that prices are in English pounds.

Triple Moon Witchware
www.witchware.com
15 Powder House Circle
Needham, MA 02492
(781) 453-0363

Winner of the Pagan Best of the Web award, Triple Moon Witchware is a one-stop shopping and information site that has everything—from profane bumper stickers to sacred herbs. You'll want to bookmark this site for the extensive information in their herbal database and for the how-to articles on correspondences and ritual ideas for sabbats. Visitors can hang out in the chat room or explore the dozens of links to other Pagan sites. Triple Moon offers a long list of packaged herbs, each listed with their magical properties. In the accessories department you'll find burners, resins, charcoal, and even herbal votive candles.

Cybermoon Emporium
www.witchcraft-supplies.com

Cybermoon offers some unique customer service perks. You can arrange layaway on orders over $50; there's free shipping to military personnel, and everyone gets a free gift with every purchase. If you are just getting started working with herbs, their Magic Herb Sets are a great way to begin. Cybermoon also carries books about herbs. Their Ritual Kits, which contain oils, incense and burner, stones, candles, and instructions, come neatly packed in carved wooden boxes. Cybermoon is a good source for obscure items such as floor sweep and black salt. They even have a currency converter for international orders.

Isis Books and Gifts
www.isisbooks.com
5701 E. Colfax Ave.
Denver, CO 80220
(303) 321-0867

Isis has a user-friendly website offering 100,000 items and tools for your "soul's journey." They offer classes in their shop, and you can also subscribe to their newsletter to learn from their expertise. In the herb department you'll find photos of the various herbs they carry in bulk—a nice touch that helps you identify what you're looking for. They also carry books on herbalism, mortar and pestle sets, and teabags that iron shut for ease in making and using your own blends.

The Blessed Bee
www.theblessedbee.com
P.O. Box 2849
Norcross, GA 30091
(770) 840-9620

Don't be put off by the angry tone in the warnings about using their toll-free number, asking for supplier's names, and the pitfalls of drinking poisonous teas. The Blessed Bee has a good selection of herbs and is helpful in describing their uses. Many of the herbs are wild-crafted and certified organic. The Blessed Bee offers free shipping for purchases over $75, gift certificates, gift wrapping, and regular clearance sales.

Cyber Magick Occult Superstore
www.cybermagick.com
PO BOX 903326
Palmdale, CA 93590
661-285-2575

Cyber Magick has a gothic slant, with gargoyles and Osiris greeting you on its splash page. They are a good source for statues and altar pieces, but they also carry loose herbs and tea blends, and some herbal books and magazines. One nice feature is they charge a flat $5 shipping fee no matter how large the order.

The Witch Shop of Eastern Pennsylvania
www.thewitchshop.net
(866) 828-0991

I found this site difficult to navigate, though it does have a decent selection of herbs. They also have a wish-list feature and printable articles on beginning Wicca. The Witch Shop carries ritual rugs and kimonos, bulk herbs, and teas. Their herbal offering kits come with a seashell, loose herbs, and instructions.

GemNAries
www.gemnaries.com
P.O. Box 505
Mays Landing, N . 08330
(866) WITCH-66

Since 1996, GemNAries has served up an eclectic blend of products. Here you'll find unusual items such as Bermuda Triangle Water for scrying, black cat bone, coffin nails, and hard-to-find herbs such as spikenard and devil's shoestring. There are articles on how to cast spells, how to use herbs, and on what toxic herbs are meant only for ritual use. You can buy cotton herbal shaman bags woven by Mayan Indians. And GemNAries carries musical instruments such as African spirit drums and guitars. Astrology is a strong component of this site with lots of information and links, free natal charts, and horoscopes.

My Witch Shop
www.mywitchshop.com

My Witch Shop has a huge selection of herbs and accessories—including exotic mushrooms, gums, resins, and Chinese herbs. If you're looking for sunflower petals, California poppy, arnica flowers, or absinthe, you're in luck. The site also lists food supplies, mills, grinders, graters, and so on. Be sure to follow the link to a database of Latin, ayurvedic, and English herb names.

Non-Pagan Herbal Shops

Global Herbal Supplies
www.globalherbalsupplies.com
Cnr. Byrnes & Eccles Street
Cairns, Mareeba, 4880
Queensland Australia
(617) 409-27781

This site has extensive botanical information on herbs. Just click on the herb name to find out facts such as medicinal uses, traditional uses, the botanical and common names, organic compounds, and a color photo. From there you can shop for the same items in the online store. True to its name, this site also carries Chinese and ayurvedic herbs.

Herbal Remedies
www.herbalremedies.com
130 West 2nd Street
Casper, WY 82601
(307) 577-6444

Herbal Remedies sells just what its name implies—herbal supplements, Chinese herb formulas, loose bulk herbs, herbal patches, teas, tinctures, and tonics. All the herbs used to prepare these tinctures are certified organic or they are wild-crafted in their natural habitat and shade-dried. Herbal Remedies has some unusual things like ashwagandha root, also known as Indian ginseng. While there are some magical herbs here, no correspondences are given.

Mountain Rose Herbs
www.mountainroseherbs.com
P.O. Box 50220
Eugene, OR 97405
(800) 879-3337

If you want your money to go toward sustainable agriculture and organic growers, check out Mountain Rose in Eugene, Oregon. They offer certified organic herbs that are free from irradiation, ozone treatment, sulfur, and other sanitary chemicals. The herbs are grown in small batches and are guaranteed fresh. A few herbs are ethically wild-harvested when not certified organic. Their Ten-Point Criteria test ensures the quality of the herbs, and they offer bulk discounts. Mountain Rose have a sister site at www.Botanical.com, which has a fully searchable database.

Stony Mountain Botanicals
www.wildroots.com
155 N Water St
Loudonville OH 44842
(419) 994-4857

Stony Mountain carries lots of extracts and blends, teas, and bulk herbs. They have unusual things like olive leaves and garcinia fruit, and various jars, grinders and mills, and capsules. Items are organized by the size of the order, which is kind of odd, but you can also search the site for exactly what you need. They have a wealth of information in the form of articles, recipes, and a newsletter.

The Herb Peddler
www.thefoodstores.com
1-888-EAT-FOOD

Part of a larger grocery site, the Herb Peddler has a large selection of dried organic herbs and sprouting seeds, a recipe section with easy ideas and tips on drying and storing herbs. If you incorporate herbs with cooking, this would be a good resource for stocking your pantry.

Craft Suppliers
Lavender Lane
www.lavenderlane.com
7337 Roseville Road Suite #1
Sacramento, CA 95842
(916) 334-4400

Lavender Lane is a great resource for do-it-yourselfers. They carry a huge supply of items for making your own incense, as well as muslin and net bags, and bottles and jars of every variety. They have a few herbal powders and resins, but Lavender Lane has a very limited supply of herbs. If you buy your herbs elsewhere, Lavender Lane is a good place to get all your accessories. Check out their library of online recipes for ideas.

From Nature with Love
www.from-nature-with-love.com

Here's another crafter's paradise. From Nature With Love is a wholesale supplier of over 1,600 ingredients for making your own products. Their extensive inventory includes hard-to-find stuff for candle and soap making or creating your own body care products. They also carry some organic herbs and seeds. Check out the range of sea vegetables, neem leaves, ground loofas, and shikakai powder. You can even get seeds to grow your own vanilla grass or Chinese licorice.

Information and Reference

Pioneer Thinking
www.pioneerthinking.com/herbs

This isn't a commercial site and there are no products for sale, but Pioneer Thinking is great for do-it-yourselfers. They have a helpful database of herbs and matching remedies, including Latin names. Visit this site to learn about herbs through articles on growing herbs indoors and how to make tinctures.

The Bear's Byte
www.thebearbyte.com

What started as the personal website of a Hopi Indian has grown to over hundreds of pages of information and instructions on working with native herbs. If you want to learn to make infusions and decoctions the old-fashioned way, this is the place. There are also many links to other sites of interest—mostly environmental pages.

Herb Research Foundation
www.herbs.org

This site is a vast storehouse of information and resources, including a specialty research library containing more than 300,000 scientific articles on thousands of herbs. The site's builders have extensive field experience in sustainable development of botanical resources. If you're looking for hard scientific information about herbs, start here.

Specialty Herb Suppliers

Pet Medicine Chest
www.petmedicinechest.com

Herbs are not for humans alone. Pets benefit from their healing properties, too. You must register to use this site, but once you have done so it is free to use. The site has a number of proprietary products for sale—including, for example, a tincture for fear of lightning. They also have a free newsletter.

MotherLove
www.motherlove.com

This site focuses on herbs especially for pregnancy and childbearing. They have good herbal information in the section under "Plants," but they don't have plants or herbs for sale. You can buy herbal products such as salves and teas here.

BARDS OF THE PAGAN WORLD

by Paniteowl

What would a festival be without vendors? How else could you find that perfect pendant, or the tie-dyed sarong, or the perfume blended just for you? Part of the excitement of Pagan festivals is finding something wondrous on good ol' vendor's row. I'm talking mystical, magical, colorful wares that are tantalizingly displayed as a feast for the eye and a balm for the soul.

If you ever have a chance to attend a festival, vendor's row is one of the most wonderful parts of it. Incense burns on makeshift altars, and aromatherapy candles glow far into the night. Trays of rocks, polished stones, and gems tempt us. Drums of all shapes and sizes lay in neat rows near the open flaps of tents draped with pennants and tapestries. Lilting Celtic melodies play a counterpoint to the deep and throbbing beat of the African

rhythms, and bells tinkle opposite the flutes and strings of East India.

Sure, there is plenty of the tacky, gross, profane, and utterly weird stuff on display. Wax gods and goddesses sit on makeshift shelves, looking down on jars of fairy dust, gaudy beaded bags, and the ever-popular cloth printed with moons and stars.

Still, we find magic here in clay figures of fairies and gnomes, in the herbalists' lotions, in paintings of unicorns and dragons. And we find it in the books—dusty old books, shiny new ones, slim volumes of poetry, and thick novels of strange lands and supernatural beings. The vendors show us things that make it possible for us to become the people we would truly like to be.

Wealth of Artistry and Information

The Pagan community has a wealth of artistry in its ranks—including silversmiths, potters, painters, sculptors, musicians, and weavers. All of them bring their talents to the festivals, ever offering us new insight through their art. Some of these masterpieces thrill us, and some make us laugh, while others show us the soul of the artist, and perhaps, even of ourselves

This is nothing new. In ancient times, the tribes would gather together to trade, barter, sell, and buy goods; but also to build relationships of trust. The same holds true today as more and more Pagan festivals and gatherings occur during the year.

At Pagan festivals, we expect to learn. We go to workshops and we search for our identity as a burgeoning culture. We expect to be accepted and nurtured. We look for magical things to decorate our houses, to adorn our bodies, to soothe our souls. On vendor's row, at the heart of the festival, stories are told, news is spread, and we can take the pulse of the community.

Many of our vendors do double duty at festivals. It has been my experience that Pagan vendors are much more than just shopkeepers or sales people. They are often the first teachers a neophyte will meet. They talk to customers and explain both the magical and mundane properties of their goods. They know where to find water, bathrooms, showers, first aid, and food. They often give classes on such subjects as tarot, runes, metal-casting, aromatherapy, essential oils, drumming, and meditation. They are often the ambassadors of good will, guiding, directing, and answering hundreds of questions.

If you want to know about a festival, or gathering, ask a vendor. They know more about what's going on in the Pagan community than anyone. They know the best places to camp, and the best places to eat. They know the gatherings that require rain gear, and the ones for which you'll need sunblock. They hear all, and sometimes, if they know you well, they'll tell all! They know the gossip and the secrets. They know the good, the bad, and the ugly. They know event organizers who are truly committed to the Pagan community, and they know those who are simply trying to make money. They are simply amazing spirits, and entirely essential resources.

I remember going to a festival in New Jersey. It was the first event this particular group had put together, and there was a bit of chaos. After a five-hour drive, my husband and I arrived to find there were no hotel accommodations nearby. After setting up our presentation tent, which was merely a screen house with a sunshade top, he left to find a place for us to stay. It was early spring, and when the clouds came in the temperature dropped to an uncomfortable 40 degrees. The wind whipped through the campground, and I found myself shivering, hungry, and thoroughly miserable. So what did I do? I went shopping, of course!

In the tents of the vendors, I found a warm pullover among the racks of tie-dyed shirts and broomstick skirts. And I found friends. The vendors had pooled their resources, and in a large tent, they had gathered a propane heater, hot coffee, snacks, and music. Warmed by the pullover, and by the vendors' hospitality, I survived the next couple of hours until my husband returned—having found a hotel more than forty miles away. That was when I realized how important the merchants were to an event's success.

The Shopping Experience

Vendors provide common space where everyone can shop to find a special stone, dress, athame, drum, or book. I understand that if I really wanted something, I could find it by surfing the Internet, or getting together with some friends for a road trip to far away cities. But to see row upon row of vendors at a gathering, offering so much that pleases us, is like being a kid in a candy store.

There should be signs posted at every festival warning people that their sales resistance can be wiped out by the magical scents, sounds, and atmosphere of vendors row. I foresee a group, Pagan Shoppers Anonymous, necessary for those dealing with the aftershock of coming home from a festival. But such is as it should be—shopping should sometimes be a completely capricious event.

For example, my love affair with magical stones began years ago when I met a vendor at a festival in New York. I had wandered into his tent and found myself attracted to a polished green stone that seemed to pulsate when I held it. I had no idea what it was, but I knew I wanted it.

However, instead of asking "How much?" I asked "What is it?" And for the next hour I listened and learned about the stone, its properties, both mundane and magical, and its history. I also learned about other stones that day, and each time I go to festival, I look to see if that same vendor is around so I can renew my acquaintance with him and learn something new.

Many of the vendors at Pagan events also have their own stores. You can find these in shopping malls, flea markets, and on the Internet. This shouldn't be surprising since the Pagan culture and community is relatively young in today's marketplace. We don't have the numbers to support a large group of merchants on a regular basis.

Most people don't realize the difficult logistics involved with being a festival vendor. They see the tents, and the merchandise on display, never realizing that the vendor may have driven twenty-odd hours just to get to the gathering. Then, after paying their fees, they have to set up their tents, unpack their goods, check the weather reports, find water, set up their campsite, and finally get a few hours of sleep before the gates open. If they are lucky, the organizers of the event have done a good publicity job, and the event is well attended. But this doesn't always pan out as planned.

For instance, a couple of years ago one festival began under clear blue skies and a warm summer breeze. The first day of the festival promised good attendance, and everyone was busy setting up and catching up with old friends. We all knew that as the weekend approached the numbers of attendees would swell, and there would be little time for socializing and such important tasks as eating and sleeping. With positive expectations, people began settling down for the night. Fires were doused, and sleeping bags unrolled, while quiet conversations whispered across the campground. Some had seen gorgeous flashes of lightning off in the distance and were enjoying nature's show. Some even danced a bit, encouraging the storm spirits to show us more. And, as often happens, we got more than we asked for.

The storm suddenly turned, heading straight for us. A spiraling fury of rain and sleet tore through the campground, leveling row after row of tents. In less than eight minutes, vendors found themselves digging out from the debris of what once were their storefronts. Twisted tent poles served as markers where

many hands searched through the mud to find items that could be salvaged. Shredded canvas lay in the fields and on the pathways. Food and clothing lay in soggy piles, and vendors knew they were in for a long, cold night of rebuilding. And rebuild they did—clearing the sites, scrounging through the piles of broken and bent tent poles to find pieces to splice together and create makeshift shelters. As dawn broke, the devastation could be seen more clearly. People made frantic runs to nearby towns to find camping gear and basic necessities. Everyone in the campground pitched in, working hard to get vendor's row up and operating, and in less than twenty-four hours the festival was back in high gear. While the losses incurred by the vendors were enormous, everyone pitched in. Some arranged for deliveries of more merchandise that same day. Some shared their stock so that others could open their shops. Supplies and monies were pooled so that all could survive the losses. Everyone knew that the only way to recoup was to open the stores. There were many innovative sales techniques used. Survival T-shirts appeared; bins of waterlogged goods were offered, and people bought them—maybe more out of a sense of contributing rather than finding a bargain. Mud-stained, water-damaged items became souvenirs, or maybe it was a way of giving a donation to those too proud to accept a gift. What came out of that experience was a sense of community, and a bonding together to survive nature's fury. No one cried "No fair!" No one whined, and no one quit. Everyone came together to rebuild and go on.

I saw no one raising prices, nor did I see anyone using the calamity as an excuse to ignore customers. They simply told the story of the storm, emphasizing that no one was seriously hurt, and thanking their deities for this blessing. They talked of the devastation as old soldiers tell war stories. And they laughed as survivors, not victims of the elements. When those of us who were there get together today the stories come out and are retold; it has become become part of the history of this new Pagan culture. And it is the vendors who carry the tale to other places, other events, and other groups of people.

So the next time you're at a festival, pay attention to the vendors. Talk to them, ask questions. You'll quickly be able to decide who are the Pagan vendors, and who are just "carnival folk."

Listen to their stories, and you'll get a clearer idea about our community. Check out their websites, visit their stores in your area. Support them, as they make their livings catering to us. And maybe, just maybe, some day we'll see the results of the vendors' efforts to help the community grow.

ALTARS, WITH A TWIST

by Laurel Reufner

Back when I was first exploring Paganism many years ago, my life needed a good infusion of humor, and this was reflected in my choice of Goddess and God statues for my first altar: Winnie the Pooh and Tigger. And this was the origins of my obsession with less-than-mainstream altar items.

My "heresies" have gotten fairly egregious though the years. I like my altars to be pleasing to the eye, a place of enjoyment, and this has meant some wild items at times.

Let's start with the altar space itself. Tons of information has already been written on where you can make an altar, many

279

of them are quite creative: from wall shelves to coffee tables, refrigerator tops, and even cardboard boxes. If your altar has a lovely surface, you may not want to cover it up, otherwise feel free to use a beautiful scarf, table runner, or even nice piece of fabric. Colors and patterns can be coordinated to reflect the seasons or your patron deities. Then there is the space behind the altar, usually ripe for any number of additions. Try hanging a pretty tapestry there. Woven-cotton tapestries can be found in any number of wonderful designs at gift stores. Eziba (www.eziba.com/StoreFront) has some lovely, though pricey, wall hangings you can use.

Another idea is to find a mask or other sort of wall icon. The website www.overstock.com has some great selections in its "Handmade: Native Cultures" section. I've seen a fanciful Buddha head for about $30, and a Tep Bronome, made in Cambodia, for a little under $40. The Tep Bronome contains the image of the goddess Apsara and welcomes guests and good spirits. Eziba also sells wall masks, including animal-inspired masks from Burkina Faso. Pier 1 Imports (www.pier1.com/home.asp) and other home decor stores are other good sources for wall masks at more affordable prices.

You can also make art the backdrop for your altar. Several options in particular suggest themselves—the first being to find a print you adore that isn't too spiritually distracting. One of my favorite sites is www.amybrownart.com, where prints start as low as $15. Check Overstock's wall art section for a huge selection of preframed art.

If you don't feel like shelling out money for a print, try making some art of your own. Create a wall hanging or collage. Or better yet, turn your kids loose. More than one creation by my preschoolers has made it to the wall behind my altar.

One final suggestion is to stick a shelf above the altar and line it with plants of a magical nature. If you can't find what you want at garden centers in your area, try Companion Plants (www.companionplants.com), located in Athens, Ohio.

Now that the altar has a backdrop, it is time to start putting stuff on the altar. My opinion is if an item has value to you as an altar item, then it's fair game. Of course, you do have to keep the concepts of clutter and chaos in mind. When things reach a point where you can no longer stand them, start figuring out what doesn't belong there any more and take it off.

A source of light for the altar is important to illuminate what it is you are doing during those nighttime rituals and to set the mood. Usually light is provided by candles placed on the altar just for that purpose, but how about using a henna lamp instead? These come in both tabletop and hanging varieties and use low-watt bulbs, so the lamps seems to glow from within. If you aren't lucky enough to have a henna supply store in your area, try a web search, as many henna websites offer the lamps.

If going electrical doesn't interest you, how about an oil lamp? These come in many different designs, sizes, and prices. On a recent walk-through of the crafts department at a local big box discount store, I found a great kit that lets you design your own oil lamp. The base cost less than $5, and it can either stand alone or nest in a clear glass vase (also around $5). The idea is to decorate the interior of the vase with flowers, shells, and the like. It can be adapted to reflect a chosen deity or pantheon.

If you really, really prefer candles and can't quite bring yourself to try something new in the lighting department, candle sconces might do the illumination trick.

If there is a particular culture or culture's pantheon that you are drawn to, your altar should try to reflect it. Even just one or two items from that culture can help you feel more connected to your chosen culture and deities. Years ago I found myself drawn to the ancient Greek pantheon, and fortunately a friend brought me back a statue of Hera from Greece, as well as a small vial of ouzo shaped like an ancient amphora. Hera became my altar's focal point, with a small bottle of olive oil on one side of her and the ouzo amphora on the other. Some stones and shells from Greece complete the effect.

Obviously, you can't always travel to distant lands to accomplish the same thing. Figure out what you can spend and focus your search on the web or at local international markets. Someone on a Celtic path might track down some mead in a small well-sealed container, and might add some peat or a stone or wooden carving made out of materials indigenous to this area.

Many Pagans, especially Wiccans, like to have some representation of the four elements on their altars. I encourage you to really stretch your imagination for this. Try using a live plant for earth, or perhaps a globe. You could go more traditional or maybe get one of those beautiful gemstone globes that are popping up everywhere. Overstock offers gemstone globes starting at $40. Fire Mountain Gems (www.firemountaingems.com) sells small globes starting at under $10. Or finally, consider stones that have special meaning, or perhaps an earthenware bowl.

Air, meanwhile, could be represented by a collection of feathers in a decorative glass or suspended like a mobile to dance in the breeze. This includes ostrich, peacock, and even the dyed chicken feathers available at craft stores that are inexpensive. Using wind chimes lets the air bring music to your sacred space. Prices on these vary widely, from $5 or $6 on up. This is one item I would prefer to buy locally, as it is always nice to hear what you are getting. Chimes can be found at garden centers, Pier 1, and similar stores. If you want to shop online, try Fire Mountain Gems or Amazon.com's garden store for some lovely chimes and customer reviews that give you an idea of what you are buying.

Representing fire offers all kinds of possibilities besides the usual candles or oil lamps. Try a chunk of obsidian. Other mineral possibilities include black onyx, so chosen because it needs to be heated ("fired") in order to turn black. Phoenix Orion has a selection of gemstones ranging in price widely. The aforementioned henna lamp can be used to represent the element of fire. And as a final idea, Overstock was offering a small tabletop chimney for just $20. Pop in a scented votive and it does double duty in engaging the senses.

For the element of water, I have three suggestions. The first idea is a small fountain, which can be purchased just about anywhere nowadays. Dollar General, or a similar store, carries some nice fountains at greatly reduced prices, and Wal-Mart and similar stores have even nicer fountains starting at around $20. Gift shops and department stores also have fountains, although the prices start to get a bit steeper. If you want to shop online, check out Amazon and Overstock to see what they have to offer.

My final water element suggestion is to buy a small birdbath for your altar. Sure, it is a bit pricier than the other suggestions, but Overstock had one standing just ten inches tall for under $30. And if you ever get tired of it on your altar, it could also be recycled out to the herb garden.

So how creative can you get with your other tools? Wands are an easy area for that. My first wand was an eight-inch length of a cinnamon stick. It worked well with my fiery nature and smelled wonderful when warmed by the altar candles. And it had the advantage of being pretty inexpensive.

I've also used dried rose stems from the times my husband has surprised me with them. Just pull off the petals when the rose is done, and then lay the remaining stem somewhere safe to dry. You can often find single stem roses for sale for around $5 or less. Red roses work well for love or general-purpose magic. Follow your intuition when choosing which to use. And if the rose was a gift, so much the better. It will be infused with the love and caring of the person who bestowed it upon you.

Feathers might also make an interesting wand. Imagine using a long, lovely peacock feather to cast your circle. While zoos are the best places to find peacock feathers, we actually found someone selling them at the local farmer's market. The cost at both places? A mere $1.

Some other useful tool ideas include the addition of a mortar and pestle for its symbolism as much as for its practical uses in preparing herbs for incense and magic uses. Small ones are cheap and can often be found a local health food stores.

Small single-cup teapots are also handy if you often drink tea or herbal infusions while in circle. And they just seem appropriate to have if you work mainly with herbs. Mine was a clearance item from Pier 1 and set me back about $10. Stores like the Dollar General offer them for

284

a couple of bucks, but make sure to check over any product completly before buying it.

For longer magical workings, I tend to keep small charms and amulets on my altar. While I try not to dwell for prolonged periods of time on the work they are supposed to be doing, they do serve as a reminder of my focus at a particular time. Tarot cards and runes can serve the same purpose. And of course, more candles and other small statues are always finding home atop the altar. These usually tend to come and go as needed.

Another couple of items that find their way onto a person's altar at one time or another are the pentacle and athame. While I've never used a pentacle, I have used flat rocks that served a pentacle-like purpose. I recently saw some lovely trays, flat bowls, and similar goodies at both Pier 1 and Overstock's native cultures area that might be useful. Some of these lovelies are $10 or less, which makes the fun inexpensive.

An athame is usually a black-handled knife, although I know few Pagans who actually own a black-handled knife for ritual use. Many have special decorative knives purchased just for ritual use. Like many other tools, these are knives that have "called" to the purchaser. As such, the cost can vary quite a bit. Other Pagans use beautiful letter openers that can be purchased much more inexpensively than special knives. And still others just grab a knife from their kitchen collection to use.

Not everyone uses an athame. Mine is a Swiss Army knife given to me by my husband for Yule several years ago. It goes everywhere in my purse and has been used for just about everything, except casting a circle. Go figure. The cost for a Swiss Army knife starts at a little under $10.

These are just a few suggestions and ideas, mind you, that will hopefully kick your own creativity into gear and inspire your sense of what is pleasing to both the spirit and the eye. Create a sacred space that you truly enjoy.

About the Authors

Elizabeth Barrette serves as managing editor of *PanGaia* and assistant editor of *SageWoman*. Her other writing fields include speculative fiction and gender studies. She lives in central Illinois. Visit her website at: http://www.worthlink.net/~ysabet/index.html.

Chandra Moira Beal is a writer living in Austin, Texas. She self-publishes books and has authored dozens of articles. She lives with a magical house rabbit named Maia.

Nancy Bennett is a poet and essayist who follows the path of the goddess. She lives on Vancouver Island. Her work has been seen in *The Blessed Bee, We'Moon, Circle,* and *The Silver Wheel.*

Boudica is the reviews editor and co-owner of *The Wiccan/Pagan Times* and owner of *The Zodiac Bistro*. She is a teacher both on and off the net and guest speaker at many festivals and gatherings. A former New Yorker, she currently resides in Ohio.

Dallas Jennifer Cobb is a work-at-home mother and author in a waterfront village in eastern Ontario. She writes about what she loves most: mothering, gardening, magic, and alternative economics. She enjoys the fruits of rural life: more time, more quiet, a contented family, and an enormous organic garden.

Ellen Dugan, a.k.a. the Garden Witch, is a psychic-clairvoyant and practicing Witch of seventeen years. She is a master gardener and teaches classes on gardening and flower folklore at a local community college. She is the author of several Llewellyn books.

Emely Flak has been a practicing solitary Witch for ten years. She is a freelance writer based in Daylesford, Australia, and works as a learning and development professional. She is dedicated to embracing the ancient wisdom of Wicca for the personal empowerment of women in the competitive work environment.

Ruby Lavender is a teacher of film studies and a freelance film critic. She is also the media coordinator for the Witches' Voice Inc., located on the web at www.witchvox.com.

Paniteowl lives in the foothills of the Appalachians in northeast Pennsylvania. She and her husband, Will, are in the process of developing a private retreat location for spiritual awareness on their fifty-six acres of natural woodland.

Diana Rajchel lives in the downtown warehouse district of Minneapolis, Minnesota. She has practiced Wicca for eight years and received a third-degree initiation in the Shadowmoon tradition in 2000. She is presently active with Twin Cities Pagan Pride.

Flame RavenHawk has been writing on the subject of shamanic Wicca and Paganism for the past fifteen years. She insists that her pseudonym is not inspired by any other authors, and any similarities are purely coincidental. Stop by Flame's Firepit at http://www.flamesfirepit.org.

Janina Renée is a scholar of material culture, folklore, mythology, ancient religion, psychology, medical anthropology, history, and literature. She is also the author of numerous popular Llewellyn books.

Laurel Reufner has been a solitary Pagan for over a decade now. She is often attracted to bright and shiny ideas. Southeastern Ohio has always been home, and she currently lives in lovely Athens County with her husband and two daughters. Her website may be found at www.spiritrealm.com/Melinda/paganism.html.

Cerridwen Iris Shea is a tarot-reading, horse-playing, ice-hockey-addicted, Broadway-dresser kitchen Witch. An urban Witch for years, she temporarily resides in the suburbs on her way farther into the woods. She is currently working on a website.

S. Tifulcrum has been a public Wiccan for more than thirteen years. With too many interests and hobbies to name at any given time, her background includes military service, clergy duties, and experience in a variety of career industries. She is happily married and the mother of a beautiful little girl. Visit her at: http://stifulcrum.tripod.com.

Get a FREE
1-year subscription
to *New Worlds*!

Inside Llewellyn's *New Worlds of Mind & Spirit*, you'll find everything you need for personal transformation. *New Worlds* is filled with articles on New Age, Wicca, Astrology, Tarot, Health & Healing, Feng Shui, Magic, Paranormal, and much more. Best of all, it's FREE for a whole year—that's six issues.

Inside each copy of *New Worlds*, you get:

- In-depth articles and how-tos by Llewellyn's expert columnists
- The scoop on hundreds of Llewellyn books, tarot decks, and many more products you can buy online or by mail
- Intimate and revealing interviews with Llewellyn authors
- Previews of the latest Llewellyn titles
- Astrology reviews and guidance
- Tarot discussion and exploration
- The latest word on witchcraft and magic
- Special offers you won't find anywhere else

To get your FREE 1-year subscription to *New Worlds*: Visit us online at **http://subscriptions.llewellyn.com**, or call us toll-free at **1-877-NEW WRLD (1-877 639-9753), Extension 8237**, or mail your request to New Worlds, P.O. Box 64383, Saint Paul, MN 55164-0383.